MAKE SUCCESS YOUR ADDICTION

DANNY RANGE

Palmetto Publishing Group
Charleston, SC

Make Success Your Addiction

Edited by Andrew Rogers
Andrew.james.rogers0461@gmail.com

Photography by Caroline O'Brien of Caroline Rose Photography
C.r.obrien112@gmail.com

Artwork by Joe Gergley
Instagram: @StrangeHumanStudios
Strangehumanstudios@gmail.com
https://www.strangehumanstudios.com/

First Edition

Printed in the United States

ISBN-13: 978-1-64111-376-2
ISBN-10: 1-64111-376-6

Danny Range is a 26-year old author, businessman, family man, life coach, and public speaker who was born and raised in Warren, Ohio. Born of two parents in their late teens, Danny recalls being homeless with his mother at fourteen, also living in a roach-covered apartment while working two jobs and participating in college classes full-time. These humble beginnings are what Danny credits for creating his work ethic, which has often been referred to as "insane" or "unheard of" by his peers.

Currently residing in Columbus, Ohio, Danny is pursuing an MBA with a specialization in Executive Management from Ashland University; he plans to use the degree to eventually open a chain of successful businesses. Danny prides himself on the fact that this book was written in one year on top of being involved in a full-time MBA program, working 60+ hours a week at an accounting job, and maintaining a social life.

Table of Contents

Acknowledgments

"When you do the right things in the right way you have nothing to lose because you have nothing to fear."

- Zig Ziglar.

Author, salesman, and motivational speaker.

I've suddenly become the guy that my peers look to for advice, yet I find myself getting the most out of life when I learn a lesson from other people. And so, I'd like to dedicate this book to the following people, who were the sole reason that I was able to do some self-reflecting and realize that I still had a lot to work on in terms of who I am as a person. Whether the advice was given three weeks or ten years ago, it all molded together at the perfect time; I believe you all deserve your recognition for it. And to the rest of you, I'm grateful for the impact you've made on me:

Thank you, Booka Booka, for giving me the happiest year of my entire life to date! You were right; I needed to balance work and play, and if there's one thing I regret it's the fact that I came to that conclusion after we went our separate ways. You deserved more of my time. I want you to know that I'm forever in debt to you for answering the phone that day. You literally saved my life. Hug Peanut for me and know that I'm still here for you if you ever need anything. I *always* will be.

Thank you, Tammy, for seeing the good in me at a time when I was going out of my way to make it hard to notice. People like you, Bryce, and the rest of that amazing family are the type of people who kept me going when I was terrified to continue pursuing all of this. I have your back, and I have your son's back, no matter what happens and no matter what you get yourselves into!

Thank you, Big Momma and Bix, for being my constant motivation. I wouldn't be alive today if I didn't care about you two so much, and I will go to the grave working to give you the life you deserve if that's what it takes. I'm a prick when it comes to money at times, but it's only because it infuriates me that you guys still don't have enough of it. I'm going to make sure you guys have it easy one day and that much I can promise.

Thank you, Grandad, for hounding me to go back to school when I swore that I didn't need to. The money from furthering my education is what will be used to promote what I love to do on the side, and you were right about the fact that I needed to make my education a priority. You always know what's best for me, and I'm *nothing* without your guidance. You're the most incredible role model I could ever hope for, and if there's one person that I owe my thanks to above all else, it's you. I can only dream to be as amazing of a family man as you turned out to be.

Thank you, Caren and Bill, for being like a second pair of parents to me. I work every day of my life while dreaming of having a family just like yours. I'll never forget you guys bringing me groceries in college when I didn't have the money for them. Thing is, you didn't know I was broke because I was an addict, and the only thing that kept me from giving into addiction completely was that constant visualization that one day I could be like you guys if I held myself together. I love you both to death! Don't ever forget it, and next time it's dinner on me for once...one day...wait, how much longer is it alright if it's on you guys?

Thank you, Dad, for taking me in when I needed it the most. I don't give you the credit you deserve for how amazing of an effort you gave to be a good father while living three hours away. I won't forget seeing your car roll up to a baseball game in the middle of Tennessee, knowing that meant six hours of driving for you on a work night, and all just to see your kid play. I know we butt heads, but it's all love! I have your back even more than you have mine. I will always be there for Nick, Meep Meep, Susie, and Lindsay as well.

Also, I can't move forward without giving recognition to the amazing people who ended up being a part of my work! I believe you must always give credit where it's due. (These links worked as of 9/26/18.)

This was the study about breaking a habit used in chapter one:

https://www.sciencealert.com/here-s-how-long-it-takes-to-break-a-habit-according-to-science

These were the techniques I mentioned I studied from Simon Sinek to learn how to properly go about public speaking:

http://confidencebuilderstoastmasters.blogspot.com/2017/04/7-public-speaking-tips-from-simon-sinek.html

This is the link to Simon Sinek's website, which gave me the idea for the entire 'why' chapter:

https://startwithwhy.com

This is where I got the Isaac Newton 'true story' from:

https://sciencing.com/first-person-discover-gravity-23003.html

This is where I found the various quotes from celebrities about the law of attraction:

https://www.fearlessmotivation.com/2017/12/07/law-of-attraction-quotes/

A direct link to the Joe Budden and Lil Yatchy argument, which inspired the chapter about controlling your waves:

https://www.youtube.com/watch?v=hmjlA4LSaN4

Any other quotes or stories were taken from prior knowledge or various search engines, and I did not intend to use that work to widen my wallet. I only included the people who have had an enormous impact on my life, those that I know can have a similar impact on others. I hope that those people can see that this was put together for all the right reasons and I do not claim the rights to their work in any way, shape, or form.

FOREWORD:

"Intro"

"Everyone has the power for greatness. Not for fame, but for greatness...because greatness is determined by service."

- Martin Luther King, Leader of the civil rights movement.

I MEAN, WOW!

You ever hear someone refer to something as a "learning process?"

Because that's exactly what my debut novel, *Warren's Finest*, was for me.

But not in the sense of it being a failure. Come to think about it, *Warren's Finest* sold roughly two-thousand six-hundred copies through the internet and in-person over the course of a year. And of those sold, I came away with proof of sale in five different countries (US, England, Canada, Australia, Ireland, and the kid in Iran said he couldn't figure out how to purchase it. But he did try, so God bless him!). Plus, it received so many five-star reviews that most of the promotional companies claimed that I was cheating, I heard from people in prison and rehab centers that claimed that I saved their lives, and I put out three-hundred and seventy-five thousand words-worth of content, without a degree in Creative Writing, in fourteen months. Lastly, writing that book gave me hope; it gave me a reason to feel like I had a purpose in life and not to implode mentally when I was a struggling drug addict on the verge of doing so…

So, no, it was not a failure. It was a learning process due to the things that it would end up teaching me about life in general, not just writing. I can't tell you how many times I made an enormous connection with a major figure in the writing industry, in business, or some type of big player in education only to have these people dig into my brand for about five seconds, see the modeling pictures with women, the swearing, the arrogance, and never so much as *consider* networking with me. The thought was to be 'loud' to draw attention to myself for publicity, and while it worked to a degree, I somehow failed to see that the only message I was sending to the world was that I dropped the drugs and discovered how to do so without getting rid of the negative qualities that I had as a person. Taking time to reflect over the past year led to me realizing that I needed to change what I'm doing with the telling of my life's story. Not that it's the best way to make connections or a ton of money, but because it's simply the right thing to do. And I've done nothing but all the wrong things with my first twenty-six years of life, so it's about time that I start heading in the other direction.

You know what else needed to change? The "Me-me-me" attitude. Everything I've done so far has circled around myself and what I wanted, also using all your praise and encouragement to pat myself on the back and push myself to grind another day, without considering how many people did or didn't get the help that they needed from my example. There's *nothing* that I regret doing more in life. (And if you didn't read *Warren's Finest*, trust me, we'll just put it simply and say that I've done a lot of regretful things...) If I was going to continue pushing with this brand, I recognized that my purpose needed to be dedicated to using my success to get people like *you* the help that you're seeking, regardless of whether that help may be in getting sober, getting motivated, etc. I want to help you achieve your goals in general! Yet, still, the question lingered: "How do I do that?"

Those of you that reached out to me through social media were aspiring business people, struggling addicts, or those who wanted to find a way to be as motivated as I am. So, what was I supposed to do? Write separate books for all of you? God, no. That would've been way too much time spent and I knew that I'd never accomplish anything in trying to promote multiple projects that had the same goal. Plus, I'm not even sober anymore. I drink casually, as I've found a way to do so without going back to my old ways. This made me feel like my focus should be on what's next for those people who lack motivation or direction, yet I just couldn't seem to find the right way to say it…

Then it clicked to me!

I may have been telling an addict to get clean, or somebody who's lacking motivation to find their drive, or giving interview advice to a young college kid who's dreaming of being the next Jeff Bezos, but essentially the advice needed to achieve any of those goals is the same. So, why don't I just combine it into one manual for you all to live by? *Ah, yes!* Don't we all *love* those little moments of clarity? That moment when you feel like a superior being has flipped the switch in your brain that gives you the exact answer you've been searching for your entire life? I knew from the moment that thought hit my mind that I needed to dedicate my life to showing everyone how to discover their "Process."

That's right, "The Process." The Process is the answer to your problems because The Process has and always will be the answer to *everyone's* problems. And don't act like you don't know what I'm talking about; we've all heard the term "Trust the Process," haven't we? Eric Thomas has screamed these exact words in hundreds of social media videos and likely in thousands of the various speeches he's given throughout his brilliant career as a motivational speaker. Joel Embiid, NBA superstar, is famous for telling 76ers fans to "Trust the Process" as his team went from the worst team to ever play in the NBA to a playoff team. Hip Hop artist Ace Hood dedicated the title of one of his many amazing mixtapes to the term "Trust the Process." Iconic entrepreneur Gary Vaynerchuk has referenced the term in many of his inspirational videos and quotes. The list could go on to create a book itself, but that's not my aim here. My aim is to point out to you that The Process has been around you your entire life and you simply didn't notice. And you won't create the life you want unless you learn it, practice it, and dedicate your life to it like I have. But let me clarify: there isn't one *specific* Process we're all supposed to follow; people like those mentioned before just preach about their own versions of it, and I just decided to combine the principles of theirs into one project and give it a name...

Throughout years of research, digging into the lives of major success stories and how they got to be where they are today, a beautiful thing called the Law of Attraction, and good old-fashioned motivation, I give to you the exact blueprint of how to reap the benefits of getting addicted to success AKA discovering your own unique Process. You'll learn how to use that blueprint to live the rest of your life happier than you ever thought you were capable of being. But know that what I meant by "success" is not in the sense of the amount of money you make, as is the common misconception of my work. Some people don't care about money, and the more I stay open-minded to understanding those people, the more I understand where they're coming from! Success—in my eyes—comes from when you achieve the one goal you've always wanted to accomplish, whatever that may be. We can all benefit from achieving a goal that we didn't believe that we had the ability to earn, as it makes us feel like we can do anything. And once we feel like we can do anything, we officially become the people who have a chance to do so as quick as a snap of our fingers.

The beautiful thing about what you'll learn in the coming pages is that it's all proven to work, as it's hard to disagree with the day-to-day rituals that made people like Ronda Rousey, Jordan Belfort, Rhonda Byrne, and Conor McGregor into the type of people that will be remembered forever, isn't it? I do realize that some of you don't look up to these people like I do, so I will also use creative writing to share stories of how the steps in this Process worked in my own life as well. And that should make it as relatable as possible, as I'm not some 'mythical figure' like those mentioned before might appear to be. *I'm one of you*, chasing my own dream of landing a major Hollywood deal for one of my future creative writing projects using the same concepts this book teaches you to use on the daily…

You know, so many people have asked me how I was able to accomplish the weight loss, getting clean, the success story, and the happiness so fast! But while the following pages will cover that full explanation, I'd like to answer it in one simple sentence that sums it up to perfection: *I made success my addiction.*

Now it's time to show you how to *Make Success Your Addiction* as well…

Are you ready to become the person that you've always wanted to be?

CHAPTER I:

MJR, Creature of Habit: Routine.

"You'll never change your life until you change something you do daily. The secret of your success is found in your daily routine."

- John C. Maxwell, author, speaker, and pastor.

Are you the type of person that feels like you have no direction in life?

I didn't mean that you need the GPS to get the grocery store, either. I meant if somebody asked you where you'd be in life within the next five years that you'd be so stressed out by the mere thought of it that you'd start an argument with the person instantly. This is the type of guy that runs through a different girlfriend twice a month and can't live in the same house for more than two years without getting uncomfortable, or the girl whose hair always needs to be a different color and if she eats the same lunch on two consecutive days her entire brain malfunctions to the point of where she may or may not remember how to turn the damn shower on.

If this is you in some form or variation, I promise you have a giant problem on your hands, but it's one that can be fixed with the content shared in this chapter. If this isn't you, the following principle will likely be something that's already a part of your life, but also something that you likely don't pay enough attention to. Your focus should be to *fine-tune it* as you read. After all, having structure in your life is the most important trait of all, as the only way you'll accomplish any type of goal without structure is by accident or by getting lucky. And you don't really want to go through life having your future dependent on luck, do you?

You sure don't! Since you don't, let's dive right into it: the way to develop that structure and see your life begin to become a lot less 'out of control' is to develop a positive addiction to being productive in a solid routine. Now, please know that it almost hurts me to write this next sentence with how plain it sounds, but it's necessary as a self-help book needs to be written out like a step-by-step manual: I like to define a routine as a schedule of daily tasks that either benefit your future or put you on a direct path towards achieving your goal. Once you've created this schedule, you stick to it every day so that you never miss a day of work, a day of exercise, the right meal, the next assignment, or whatever it is that you want to make sure that you always remember to stay on top of. In time, doing the right things over and over leaves you no choice but to find yourself in a better place. And once you see these incredible results, developing an addiction to them will end up being the easy part of the Process. Now, since I'm still trying to process the fact that I, as a creative writer, had to seriously write a sentence as plain as the one I just did, I'm going make up for it by giving you the perfect example of what a good routine is through a story…

It's one of a man very close to me, one who happens to be my role model, and the same one who taught me everything I know about how to climb my way up the ranks in business, how to develop a unique relationship with each family member that I have, and how to be a respectable man in general. He's the guy who has the swagger to become the big voice in any room while sitting across from any man, and the one whose signature Michelob is always made ready for him at any event that he graces his presence with. He's the same man who found the motivation to work so hard at the end of a forty-year career that the company he managed offered him three times as much money as he'd made in his *entire career* just to get *three more months out of him!* It's a real-world rags-to-riches story, but not one that you can see on a big screen; he's too humble to accept all the attention that he rightfully deserves.

That man of the hour is Malcolm J. Range, my grandfather.

Many of you know my story of being raised by a single mother, but the next greatest gift I was given was being born into the Range family. The Range brothers were all self-made multi-millionaires by the time I came out of the womb. Their money isn't mine, and I wouldn't want it anyway, but I admit that being raised by my mother in a household without money yet having access to the guidance of millionaires became the perfect storm. I'd have the drive from not being raised in a household where I could be spoiled and wanting better for my future children, all while being able to ask the people who had money the exact steps that I'd have to take to acquire my own. Now, we're not talking about people who were handed some inheritance and can't spell the word 'stress' or anything. We're talking hard-nosed, hard-working men that were raised in the rough part of Brooklyn, New York. 'Tough guys' who moved to Warren, Ohio without a dime in their pockets before they became the people that you'd want to take financial advice from.

The brothers paid their own way through schools like Kent State University and Youngstown State University, amongst others, where they hitch-hiked to school with old clothes on their backs, slicked-over hair, and testy looks on their faces to get their business degrees. Malcolm J graduated from Youngstown State and swept the floors for pennies at a company I won't name here while attending the institution. Upon graduation, this handsome, blue-eyed man used his business degree to get a real job with the same company he used to sweep the floors for, then he hustled his way up to being president of that company as the new janitor swept the floors for him after he called it a day. He'd go on to use the money he made there to invest in stock from multiple companies that went on to be worth millions, as well as opening Range Inc, an investment company that bought into multiple fast-food restaurants that you've likely been to hundreds of times.

Now no, no, no, don't think of that story as a guy who worked hard in college and then just got some high-paying job that allowed for lucky investments in stocks that made him some undeserved millionaire that you all should envy. How do you think somebody like that works their way up? You think every day was easy? That he had no direction, but he kept showing up and one day he was just handed the promotion that somebody else deserved?

Not even close.

He woke up at the same time every day, wore the same pair of black socks on Monday, then the same blue pair on Tuesday, and the same white pair on Wednesday. He ate the same breakfast at 6:05 AM and drank the same coffee at 6:45 when he got to work. He left after saying bye to the same secretary after putting forth the same insanely productive effort that he put in the day before and went home to sit in the same seat at the same dinner table where his family was waiting for him to—

Hold up!

Did you catch that?

"Catch what? The part where your grandfather does the same stuff all the time?"

Sighs

Well, that's obviously part of it. But did you catch the part where I mentioned that he was always "insanely productive?" Now, maybe this is the case for you and at one point in my life this pertained to me but being 'insanely productive' is probably this thing that your brain tells you is when you put forth such a miraculous effort that you're either physically or mentally exhausted at the end of the action. Although, my grandfather's routine offers an easy cheat to that thought for you guys: being insanely productive may take a ton of effort, but if being insanely productive is something that you've done at the exact same time and on the exact same days, then it becomes just another part of your life and not something that takes extra effort to bring about!

When you wake up in the morning and relieve yourself in the bathroom, do you think twice? No, you do it every day. When you take a shower after the gym, do you really have to remind yourself that you're dirty or do you practically float to the shower because you're so used to it? You float there, or if you're not David Blaine and you can't float there, then you at least jump in without thinking too much into it. So, when I tell you that you can float like David Blaine to the gym and lift weights as hard as you possibly can, or that you can float to the office and shred a thirteen-hour shift like it's nothing, or that you can drive home without stopping at your drug dealer's house like it's nothing, I'm saying that you can! And you can do so easily, but only if you manage to get through the first grueling month of getting used to doing so...

Just process that last sentence for a minute! *One month* is all it takes to break a habit, which in this case would be you living your life in a way that doesn't allow you to accomplish your goals. Now this claim is from my own experience, but it's also been medically examined and debated amongst highly decorated, intelligent individuals for decades. An insanely popular book from the 1960s called *Psycho-Cybernetics* was written by a man named Maxwell

Maltz, a plastic surgeon whose patients showed him that it only took about twenty-one days to get used to their new face! I don't know about you, but if I wake up in the morning and go to brush my teeth, then look up and see that I now have the face of a thirty-year old black man, that's going to cause me to scream at the top of my lungs. But I guess it doesn't sound so bad if it only takes twenty-one days to get used to (I think). And I also think this will go without saying at this point, but if twenty-one days is all it takes to get used to having a different face, then do you seriously believe that it'd be such a tough task to adjust to not smoking cigarettes or something along those lines? According to Maltz's logic, if you adjust the way you live your life to accomplish your goal, it shouldn't even take the full twenty-one days because it's likely a lot less shocking than a new face. Also, for those of you who, by some small chance that's not even able to be calculated, are reading this with a new face and getting used to it was your goal, then it sounds like you're in luck, my friends! Twenty-one days and counting!

I did say this topic was highly debated, though. In 2009, researchers from University College, London looked at the habitual lives of ninety-six different people over the span of about twelve weeks. They claimed that, according to their research, it took about sixty-six days for these people to get used to their new habits. In this article, those same researchers also said that the results varied from only eighteen days to a much longer two-hundred and fifty-four. But still, let's look at this from the optimistic perspective: let's say you're one of those people that will take as long as possible to adjust to what it takes to chase the goal, and you're trying to conquer the hardest habit of all, which I consider to be drug-addiction. It will still only take you less than an entire year to get used to your new life! That's the life you're dreaming of having while you read this and the life you keep picturing that probably inspired you to pick up this book. So, what's a little less than a year of adjusting to something new if it allows you to accomplish what you dream of accomplishing every day?

If you get like grandpa MJ and find your own productive routine, you will get so used to dream-chasing that it will feel weird *not* to do all that dream-chasing. In terms of the step-by-step on how to develop your schedule, we'll physically leave space for you to develop one later. But I want you to start thinking about these important questions, so you have a general idea of what to fill that schedule with once you get there: What's your schedule like? Do you work at the same time every day? What do you do after work? Do you work late at night? Ok, so what do you do in the morning before work and in the evening after? Know that the key is to fill this schedule with things you love to do, so you don't get sick of doing the same things over and over. And if there is a part of your day that you don't like doing but that you must do, you need to make sure that the other daily tasks make you so happy that you won't mind going through it because you always have something to look forward to afterward. My grandfather used that routine to acquire enough wealth to take care of his entire family, while he was alive and long after death, and it even allowed him to do so well before death was even a thought. That's the type of success you'll see with your own goal-chasing, so long as you develop that structure using a routine/schedule of your own.

The schedule never stops, even after you accomplish the goal; you simply pick a new goal and re-write the schedule in a way that attacks that goal as well. MJ is retired now; the guy still wakes up at the same time he used to for his old job, without an alarm clock and for no reason. I've never seen anything like it! I slept in until 8 AM the last time I stayed at his place and he said, "Well, Jesus, you trying to sleep the entire day away or something, Danny? What the hell is the matter with you?" in that hysterical Brooklyn accent when I got to the top step with bedhead. I even drove to his house for dinner that same weekend and got there a minute late at 5:31 PM. Yes, one entire minute. That's one sixtieth of an hour, one sixtieth, and as I reached for my phone to check the time because he always beat it into my head that nobody respects a guy who's late all the time, I noticed that he had called me to see where I was at 5:30! *The routine times are engraved into his brain!*

No remorse at all, man. I'd like to imagine he shook his head and called the millisecond the clock hit 5:30. After sixty seconds late, he likely started shaking his head harder, staring at my spaghetti as if it was going to get cold or some shit while wearing his routine polo shirt with that grey head of hair slicked over. This all because he's gotten so used to being on time and dealing with people who are never late that he couldn't process why my pea brain didn't also see that as a critical mistake. Hold on, he wouldn't let me live with this, so let me clarify that I said before that he wakes up for no reason because he doesn't have to wake up for an official job in retirement, but he actually gets up to check his stocks that are still soaring, along with the revenue from his restaurants that I refer to as 'money factories' as he makes more in that relaxing retirement than most people will ever dream of making in their entire lives. There's always a new goal; there's always a new dream to chase for him. That can be you as soon as you open your mind to adjusting your lifestyle however it needs to be adjusted.

If you've ever wondered how somebody can go from nothing to something, even from nothing to everything, just remember that I once asked a self-made millionaire from the streets of Brooklyn that same question; his response was that I needed to develop a routine before I did anything else, and that's exactly why I started this book off by giving you that same advice. But I'd like to imagine some of you may be thinking to yourself, "What if I get sick of doing something like this and there's absolutely nothing that I can do to change that? Is there another way for me to get where I want to be, Danny?" To get tough on you: no, this is how you need to do it. Stop running from the answers to your problems just because the road there seems like it's filled with gigantic roadblocks that you don't think you can drive around. Become the type of person who doesn't shy away from a tough fight and watch as being that type of person starts to make every fight in life a little less difficult to win. But to some of you thinking that way, and to the benefit of those who aren't, there is, in fact, another 'cheat code' that can make the uncomfortable part of this a little less tough to deal with…

Simply ask yourselves my favorite question in the world because its results should be downright magical...

That is, only if you want to accomplish your goal badly enough…

"*Why* do you want to achieve this goal?"

CHAPTER II:

Why: Find the Fire

"The starting point of all achievement is desire."

Napoleon Hill, author of *Think and Grow Rich*.

So, YOU *FINALLY* gave it a chance!

You took in all that information from the first chapter and attempted to develop an amazing routine that does nothing but push you towards achieving your goals. But let's fast forward for a moment: you're now a few weeks into getting used to that routine, and that magical feeling of motivation that you felt at the beginning of all this is fading like LeBron's hairline, as you start to feel it creeping up your neck...

"It?"

Yes, IT! The damn clown from that horrifying movie, except this one doesn't have a corny outfit or target children. In fact, the only thing he has an interest in is you, which is practically a death sentence, and the timing of it couldn't be worse! Jesus H., you had just picked up a life-changing book and everything. Just your luck, right? Wait, my bad, that's not where we're going with this and I promise it'll be the last time I halt your progress with my own anxiousness to get back to writing about demented things. Any who, what I meant by "it" creeping up your neck is that devil in our ear that we all experience, no matter who we are, where we're from, or what goal we're pursuing. It's the devil in the form of temptation AKA an enormous wall to all your beautiful progress that's so big Donald Trump himself would have to admit that it would likely cost more than he originally intended...

You may have heard this sinister voice in the back of your cranium when you're in the gym: "You know what Billy? You've exercised enough; you don't have to do cardio today! Go home and eat a pizza like the obese man you're meant to be...what's life without a few slices of that scrumptious, cheese-filled crust, you know?" It's that same little voice that all addicts are terrified to hear from: "Nah Susan, it's all good! You've taken three weeks off from drinking and proven that you don't need it every day. Obviously, there's no addiction here! I don't see a reason why you couldn't slug a couple of cold ones. Like, come on, you only live once!" Then, next thing you know, Susan's shirt is the bathroom while she's on top of the bar screaming, "*You only live once!*" at the top of her lungs. And lastly, which happens to be my absolute *least* favorite of them all, the previous voice's ugly cousin that whispers in your earhole after you've started to see some incredible results: "Nah, it's ok Danny. You're never going to be the richest man in the world, and you *do* need to live a *little bit*. Take a few days off and relax! Don't overwork yourself, homie. We all deserve some 'me' time!"

I can't stand it!

It's impossible to avoid hearing it as temptation is just a part of human nature, so don't feel alienated if you feel like you hear your voices more often than other people claim to hear theirs. If you thought you weren't destined for greatness or destined to accomplish your goal because you've heard this voice, you need to throw that thought right in the trash and never dwell on it again. Know that there's a beautiful way to negate these negative thoughts, and it comes in the many different variations of the question I ended the last chapter with. I want you to start monitoring this voice of temptation that lingers in your mind, and each time you notice that you start to hear it, stop whatever you're doing and ask yourself this question: "*Why* do I want to accomplish my goal so badly?"

But there's a tweak to this. Let's say that you're the type of guy/gal that wakes up in this great, big world and struggles to find the motivation that seems to come naturally to others, then you look in the mirror and ask yourself that magical question I've introduced you to only to realize that your answer is something along the lines of, "I guess I don't have a good reason, actually. You know what? That must mean this goal isn't worth the effort that comes with accomplishing it. I think I'll go ahead and smoke a doobie today while I watch Family Guy, instead of doing something productive. By the way, how does one apply for unemployment?" Then yeah, you're going to have to add some extra weight to that magical question for it to have a powerful effect on you…

And I almost skipped to this part when writing the book, I swear to God. It's incredible once you realize how to use it the right way, like somebody put a giant red button on your hand that says, "Keep me going," and all it takes is a slight touch of the pinky to get it working. Just imagine being able to unleash an unstoppable animal in the realm of self-motivation that you never realized that you had. But you must understand that there's a big difference between the guy that feels good when he loses weight because he wants to look better on his next date, and the guy who feels like he didn't accomplish enough after he lost that weight because he *knows* that he has a reason to strive for bigger things. That second guy is capable of anything and believe me, the rest of this chapter is a key piece in helping mold you into guy number two. What better information to provide to you than something that is proven by highly successful people like Simon Sinek to work time and time again?

Haven't heard of Simon Sinek?

Neither had I, until I booked my first public speaking gig at a rehab center and found myself hyperventilating with excitement in my father's basement, while I hoped the people who I'd be giving life advice to would never find out that I was still mooching meals and rent from the man who gave me birth. Suddenly, and only after the shaking in my hands and knees had ceased, it dawned on me that I didn't have the slightest damn clue about how to give a speech to a public audience! Those two words popped into my mind, red lettering and all, just like the signs they put up at all their events: *Ted Talks*. I'd spend the next two hours scouring their site, Youtube, and Google for good examples of speeches. Not just any speech, though; I was determined to find a certain somebody giving that speech, somebody whose talk would inspire me so much that I'd want to study their every move, and then I'd research how they went about putting that speech together.

Not only did my little fingers find the right speech, but I hit the gold mine. A link on Youtube would send me to TedxPugetSound, which was an event in 2009 where this man named Simon Sinek gave a talk called "Start with why—how great leaders inspire action" based on a concept he had written a book about. Wearing dorky glasses and a button down shirt with cheap-looking jeans, I was almost as blown away by how normal he looked as I was with how professional his delivery sounded. Four million views though, I thought. If a man that looks no more superior to others than I do is able to sound far more superior with knowledge, then a little research has got to be able to allow me to do the same, right? Maybe I really *can* do this!

I dug into who he was like a mafia hitman who needed to hide a body in the desert within the next half hour, and I dug even harder than that hitman into how Simon was able to speak so fluently. Little things that he recommended from a few articles on the internet sold me, as they were fundamentals that were so simple, yet I never would've assumed to be necessary if I took a swing at my first speech without any of this research involved. Things like don't talk right away, so that the audience won't assume that you're nervous, but also to show that you're in complete control on stage. I also came to find that Simon's book *Start With Why* was a number one bestseller that had thousands of reviews on Amazon. Sinek went on to release another successful book called *Find Your Why*, and by then I realized that there was no point in further researching his ideas; the fact that he was able to make two books become an easy sell based on one similar-sounding idea let me know that I had found something special. The first book is all about leadership, leaders in business and how those leaders can inspire the people who work for them. It all comes down to 'why,' putting the reason for doing the work *before* the work itself. The more I thought about it, it couldn't have made more sense, then my heart dropped when the previous sentence made me realize something…

I had heard this before, many times, and it was through various quotes by other people as successful as Simon or even more so. What's so amazing about it is there are too many success stories that have mentioned some variation of this concept to quote here, but it wouldn't be right if I didn't for a few of them, and so I will. (I have got to save the trees, you know? I already killed too many of them with my first book. Short and sweet, Danny. Make it short and sweet.)

"When your *why* is big enough you will find your how." - Les Brown, author and motivational speaker.

"*When you find your why*, you find a way to make it happen." - Eric Thomas, author and motivational speaker.

"The two most important days in your life are the day you are born, *and the day you find out why.*" - Mark Twain, entrepreneur and writer.

Whoa, I thought, it's not exactly *what* goal you're trying to accomplish that's so important; it's *why* you feel like you need to better yourself overall, also *why* being the best version of yourself is so important to the well-being of those around you. Just think about it for a second: you picked up this book because you want to accomplish a goal or get over some type of hump in your life, but *why*? Why exactly do you want to do that? What are you trying to prove? And no, I don't mean to me; I don't mean 'what are you trying to prove to the world,' either. *What are you trying to prove to yourself?* Why do you want to be in a better place? Is that a good enough reason to fire you up so much that you'll stop at nothing until your goal is smashed, buried, crucified, and you crushed it yourself with nothing short of a borderline-insane work ethic, all while sporting a great attitude while you did so? If not, then your why simply isn't good enough. Case closed!

But that doesn't mean you can't find a better one…

Think about what really matters to you and to be more specific, what causes you the most pain? Yes, I said pain. *What has hurt you the most in life?* What part of your life do you want to get rid of the most? For me, it was the financial struggles for my mother's family. And today is the best example I could ever give you, as I write this on Christmas Eve having just spent an awesome night with my father's wife's family. I love those people and they treat me like their own; I admire them beyond belief for that, but we all know that it's not the same to spend a holiday with people you're not related to. Well, it's better to say that I *hope* you don't know what that's like! It's hard not to look around and be reminded that I can't spend Christmas with my mother and brother because we don't all live in the same city. We can't go to some family gathering because there isn't one to go to. I go to another family's party and am reminded of the fact that I don't have enough money to provide a place for my mother to live close to me or to send my brother to college at a school that's close enough for us all to be together...

Do you have any idea how much pain that causes? My eyes light up like fire as I type this, while the hair stands up on my arms in frustration. But I don't let that anger lead to some sort of depression; I let it light a spark underneath me, a spark that pushes me to work harder so that I don't ever have to experience a night like this again. It's similar with what Simon says (no pun intended): I recognize the benefit of putting thought into the reason why I do things before I think about how I do them. I'll let tonight motivate me through 2019 until I make this year the most productive of my entire life, so that next Christmas Eve is different...

Just to really put my point in perspective: I wrote that paragraph in December 2018, and I'm writing this one in 2019 having landed a high-paying job well above my experience level, while I already booked four speeches for 2019 at a major University and multiple high schools. I got accepted into an MBA program and now I'm about to turn this book in a year ahead of schedule, as providing money for my family has become the least of my problems. Do you see how beneficial this thought process can be for you? Imagine what you can accomplish in the next few months if you find a good enough reason as to why you need to put in more work. Think about what gets under your skin. What causes you pain to the point of holding back the tears? Do you want to show your ex that you can do better than them? Do you want to provide a better life for your family, like I do? Do you want to become an actress to show your parents that they're idiots for telling you that it was impossible?

Ah, then *now* you've found your why.

Let it be the reason you wake up earlier because it gives you a better chance at success. Let it be the reason that you save that last two hundred dollars left over from your check instead of spending it on shoes or Grey Goose. Let it be the reason that you strap on that uniform and go out there to play the game again, even after you just had the worst game of your entire life while your girl was flirting with the stoner from Geometry class that you can't stand. Once you've applied this thought to the low points of your routine, you'll watch as you develop the drive to work harder at accomplishing your goals than any man or woman you've ever met…

Isn't it ironic how you've gone through your entire life dreading things like break ups, financial struggles, failure, and all because you were taught that they are the worst type of things that can ever happen to you? When really, if you look at those things the right way, *they can turn out to be the reason that you got to where you wanted to be in life.* So, now you have that fuel for the fire, and you have a routine to apply that fire to. But why allow there to be any bad days? The first two chapters of this book may sound like it's all work and no play, but what if I told you I had the ability to turn your work into play? What if I told you I could teach you how to get as fired up for Monday morning as you likely do for Friday nights?

Know that ninety-nine percent of the world slumps their shoulders on Monday morning, then they slurp their coffee, sigh, and complain about their lives while they dream of Friday night. The one percent shows up at work on Monday morning smiling wide, they have a spring in their step, they're excited to experience each day of the week because they love their lives, and there's no need for caffeine because they always wake up before the alarm clock goes off. I'm proudly part of the one percent, but it's not because of money; it's not because I dropped the drugs. *It's because I found something to live for.* And when I introduce you to the concept in the next chapter, I can promise you that you'll find yourself falling into the one percent as well...

Let's find your passion.

CHAPTER III:

Turn the Light Bulb On: Find Your Passion

"The only way to do great work is to love what you do."

Steve Jobs, founder of Apple.

HAVE YOU EVER had anybody ask you what the craziest experience of your entire life was?

For most people, this question has a lot of hype behind it; they'll ask it and expect one of the most interesting stories they've ever heard in return. I bring this up because it's a question that's been asked to me more times than I could realistically count, having lived the life of an addict who began experiencing life on the edge at only fifteen-years old. I find the question comes mostly from people who've read my first book, who were fascinated by its intensity and want to know as much about how and why it happened as they possibly can. Now I'm big on body language, as it tells more about a person's intentions than words could ever hope to, and what stands out most to me about the people who ask this question is that they carry themselves as if they're intimidated to even ask it in the first place. It's almost as if they're horrified to hear the answer, but they can't stop themselves from asking it for the life of them! You should see the looks on their faces when my immediate response shows that it doesn't require meditation, that it's genuine, and it's the exact *opposite* of what they're expecting to hear...

The introduction of our next principle will come in the form of the most incredible day of my life, but not a day that I've ever put to paper before, and not one that happened at 3 AM during some pointless, wild binge. This story happened on January 4th, 2016 and began at approximately 7:30 AM. Wearing a button down dress shirt that did its best to wrap around my flabby chest, obesity was somehow finding a way to make me sweat despite the thirteen-degree weather on a routine freezing morning in Columbus, Ohio. As I cruised down Route 71 towards my day job where I worked as an underachieving accountant, I could feel my fingernails digging through the steering wheel as I gripped it, hyperventilating like someone just told me that my child had been raped. The withdrawals from the drug habit I had kicked just thirty days ago were still in full effect, while I pondered what my next step was in life. My eyes drifted to the left where a good-looking woman passed me by in a Mercedes SUV; I wondered how long she would last if the devil made her walk a week in my shoes...

Something that a lot of you may not know about addiction is that putting down the drug itself isn't the hardest part by a long shot. Those of you who haven't experienced it don't understand how hard it is to change the way you live your day-to-day life, in terms of how you speak, who you hang out with, and how you think. The devil's snow made me feel like I had a purpose, like I had a reason to get up in the morning. I could earn money to get more of it; I could get through that tough winter morning because I had getting high to look forward to. But without it I was just going through the motions. I wouldn't wish the gut-wrenching feeling of a meaningless existence on anybody; I just couldn't believe I had come to the point of where I envied the woman driving next to me for no reason, like she was public enemy number one for having her life together. I spent that day of work staring through the computer screen, but one thing I promised myself was that I wouldn't continue to let this Debbie-downer thought process plague the rest of my life. I can recall sitting on the toilet in our office's public restroom while clasping my hands together in prayer, hoping someone above would give me all the answers.

By the time I got off work, the sun had dropped behind the clouds to cast shade over the city of Columbus as I exited my vehicle to enter my kickboxing gym without any rap music blaring. The silence was more alarming than a booming sound system could ever hope to be since the personal trainers had grown accustomed to it being a part of my daily entrance. I pushed through the glass door of 9Round Fitness with shoulders slumped and a pair of aviator sunglasses covering my tired eyes, while the upbeat voice of the trainer working caught my attention…

"Sheesh!" said Miles. "No ghetto music today, my man? What, did the Cavs lose? LeBron isn't leaving you guys already, is he?"

Despite seemingly being seconds away from becoming the slickest wrist-cutter in town, that last question drew a smirk onto my face, and I looked upward to see the trainer I called "Mr. Steal Your Girl." Miles was his real name, and even though the layout of every 9Round gym contains all-black gym bags pressed up against brick walls painted black themselves, the kid had a glow to him that lit up the room. He was only nineteen-years old, already an entrepreneur with his own personal training business, and he sported a perfect smile with the abs of Brad Pitt in the movie *Troy* to accompany bright blue eyes. Now on top of being fat, I lacked confidence at the time, so I gave him the nickname because I'd take notice to how every girl walking in would drool at the sight of the kid with a hypnotized look in their eyes. You know, while they all ignored me… You had to hear the quotes from the girls when they saw another trainer was working: "Wait, is the other trainer working at all? I was kind of hoping he did..." Then the other trainer, my buddy, Eli, would respond, "Let me guess, you mean the pretty one, right?" "Uh, yeah, Miles! Where is he?" But I have got to give it to the kid: *he was completely humble about it!* A class act, with a positive personality that I dreamt of having at the time…

"Nah, man. Luckily for me, one of the only bright spots I have right now is my Cavs." I tossed my bag down along with head, as I began to wrap my hands for class. "Just not my day, I guess."

"It's all how you look at it, man!" Miles said, slapping my shoulder and then backing up a step to cross his arms. "You have so much going for you, why spend any day depressed?"

A shrug of the shoulders was all he got in response, while the wrapping of my hands continued. Miles didn't walk away but had gone to his phone as an awkward reaction when he realized that I wasn't going to respond. And to this day, I can't tell you why I did it, but my next move was intuitive: I turned around to look at the kid before I had a chance to think about why I was doing so. He was angled in a way that allowed my eyes to be drawn directly to his phone screen; I noticed that he was on Instagram with the screen showing his profile, *which had 20K followers and counting!*

"Hold up," I said, dropping a hand wrap and scooting close enough to physically grab his phone from him. His eyes shot at me fast as lightning, with an alarmed look on his face. "My bad, man. *I just noticed you're fucking social media famous!* How does one attract that much attention to themselves? Let me guess, it's from all the girls that magically flock to you in your everyday life, lucky little shit!"

"I wish it was, man!" Miles returned, shaking his head in laughter. "No, but it's all hard work and dedication. Actually, I can't even let that conversation die right there; didn't you say you were writing a book?"

"Trying to."

"Right, well don't get down about that because I wouldn't have a clue about how to start one of those!" He whispered, rolling his eyes. "Why I asked is because this is a process I'm using. Step-by-step and if you stick to it, which I know you can because you have a lot of dedication in you, you can easily attract attention to you for that book of yours!"

Class had started now, but the other wrap still laid lifeless on the floor while I became infatuated with learning how to start building a page like his. The hilarious part about what happened next is seven people stared at us, as we continued this conversation for the next fifteen minutes while they had to go through the first few rounds of class by themselves. Their trainer was showing all the signs that this wouldn't end up being his permanent gig! He ran through all the steps necessary to begin, whilst I asked question after question about what worked and what didn't. That is, of course, until the following conversation introduced me to a thought that would end up changing the entire course of my life…

"You'll do well with it, man!" Miles claimed, tapping my shoulder again with the always crystal-clear smile. "You just have to have tough skin, that's all. Understand that a lot of people are going to hate on you for no reason, like you're a bad person for having the audacity to believe in yourself, you know? A lot of them just don't plain care about what you have to offer, too. If you can get used to that, shake it off, and keep pressing, it works!"

"Well, of course they wouldn't care if my profile is all about selling a book to them. Why would they give a shit about some random guy's book?" I asked, as Miles shrugged his shoulders to signal that he agreed with the way that I worded the question. "People don't care about some guy's story, you know?"

"But they will care if that guys story has something to offer them."

When he said it, he walked off to teach the class, so he could keep his job and all. (Not a bad idea, right?) But I didn't join the class like he expected me to; I stood in place while that last sentence soaked into my brain. While it was soaking, it happened to drizzle its magic all over the exact nerves that I wished had been working for years. I had forgotten that my first passion was always to help other people in whatever way that they needed helped. Drugs made me forget that side of me, but that conversation going the way it did, and having my book mentioned in the same light made it dawn on me: I didn't have a passion in life at the time, but I could *create* one. I could use my story to help other people, not just to brag about how unique my upbringing was. And while techno music blared above my head, while the people around me did their best to shed some pounds after work, I began to peer out the window of the gym into the dark of the night and feel a powerful feeling of hope flow throughout my veins. The gym would be there another day, but I had more important matters to tend to. I reached down and grabbed my bag, forgetting to grab the other wrap while the first one was still wrapped around my right hand and jetted out the door to head home and begin chasing my dream...

"Wait a second!" Miles barked from the other side of the gym, as he lunged towards my hand wrap and proceeded to toss it to me like I couldn't just grab it the next day. "You forgot one, my man!"

"Oh shit," I said, dropping my head in laughter. "Appreciate you!"

As he handed it to me, he paused before he ran back to teach his class. Smirking now, while cocking his head back to signal that he already knew the answer to this coming question: "The light bulb just went off, didn't it?"

You're damn right it did, Miles...

I went home that night and dug into how to build a brand, also the best way to sell a book, which lead me to discover that public speaking and writing go hand and hand. I spent that night and the next researching motivational speakers, then decided it would take more than one bullet to stop me from becoming one myself. On January 6th, 2016, I posted a photo of a cat looking into a puddle with its reflection showing a grown tiger, and the caption above it said, "Believe in yourself." The caption on that photo became the public announcement that I was going to make storytelling my life, also that I was going to begin working on getting completely sober for an extended period. And as I sit here typing what is close to becoming my 400,000th word of published product, I proudly say that the rest is history!

That's exactly how it happened: no exaggeration involved. I made motivation, positivity, and storytelling a part of my everyday routine, and it gave me a reason to wake up happy on Monday morning. It gave me a reason to almost dread Friday night; my work week is more exciting to me than the weekends because I do what I love every day. Even when I'm at work, I *stay* motivated because business is the driving force that makes the paid advertising part of my dream possible. And now *you* have a solid schedule, you have a reason to stick to that solid schedule like your life depends on it, but you've got to start thinking about what you really want to do with your life to officially enjoy *living* that life! Tony Robbins loves changing people's lives for the better. Oprah loves sharing the newest book with her beloved audience. What do *you* love to do? Is it a part of your everyday life? *Why not?* Are you *sure* that you can't find the time to make your passion a part of your life?

And if you're struggling with what you want to do with your life, I want to take the time to tell you to stop kidding yourself. Let's do an exercise: I'm going to ask you this question and I want you to be honest about the answer. When I ask you, "What do you want to be?" What is the first thing that comes to your head? Don't tell me that you said you wanted to be a nurse, when really the answer was that you wanted to be a rock star and then you created four reasons pertaining to why you can't be one, so you settled for nursing school. That person doesn't want to be a damn nurse; the only reason they won't become a rock star is because they *choose* not to! If you are in nursing and you want to be a rock star, your routine should consist of going to your nursing job and then going home, taking care of your errands, and spending your free time looking into how you can become a rock star. Remember, we don't want to be the ninety-nine percent; we want to be part of the one percent because the one percent lives life the way that they should, and that's by doing what they love. If you're this nurse I'm referring to, then know that infinite happiness can be on its way as soon as you start rocking out, while anybody's meaningless negative opinion about you doing so gets tossed in the trash where it belongs. Don't be the person snarling at the guy who loves the life he lives, *be the person the naive are snarling at.*

But while my own example seemed like it happened overnight, I want to make sure that you understand that it didn't. As sad as it sounds, I struggled for months to discover how to enjoy what was a very rewarding and happy life that I had created for myself because I was terrified to officially let go of some of the 'harmless' things I loved about who I used to be. I'd like to imagine that there's likely some parts of your previous life that you're afraid to let go of, too. Just know that change may be terrifying, but the more we embrace change, the more we find that the things we're afraid to let go of are often the *only* things left in life that are holding us back from becoming the happiest and richest versions of ourselves.

Do you fear change?

Don't.

Because once I show you the benefits of embracing it, you'll see that this entire process begins to feel like it's smoothing itself out, rather than coming across as a bumpy road that blows your tires out.

(Unless you're from Youngstown, I guess. I can't help you guys with all the potholes, sorry.)

CHAPTER IV:

Change: Step Out of Your Comfort Zone

"You're always one decision away from a totally different life."

Mark Batterson, New York Times Best-Selling author.

HAVE YOU EVER heard of the phrase "Step out of your comfort zone?"

Just look at the type of people who know the importance of this practice...

"Move out of your comfort zone. You cannot grow if you're not willing to feel awkward when trying something new." - Brian Tracy, author and public speaker.

"Once you step out of your comfort zone your life begins." - Uriah Hall, UFC fighter.

"Life begins at the end of your comfort zone." - Neale Donald Walsch, author, actor, and speaker.

"I constantly get out of my comfort zone. Once you push yourself into something new, a whole world of new opportunities opens up." - Terry Crews, actor, author, and the 2017 Time Person of The Year.

But what is a 'comfort zone?'

It's not our fluffy bed that we don't want to leave in the morning, or the heated car seats we don't want to take our keister out of as we sit outside of our job not wanting to go in at 6 AM. *It's not even a physical place at all!* Your comfort zone is in your mind and it's one of the worst burdens that our amazing God has placed upon us, as it's completely out of our control. How can we control a way of thinking that comes naturally to us, right?

But really, the best way to explain what a comfort zone is would be by telling the story of a kid I know, one I've known my whole life, and one that probably has a lot in common with a lot of people you know. Now this kid, who we'll call Dick (I'm completely immature, I know. Just keep reading) has it all. Dick has eyes as blue as the sky on a day where the clouds decided to ask for paid time off, he's in shape, he drives a luxury vehicle that most his age only dream of driving, and everyone says he's naturally as funny as Kevin Hart when he does stand up. What those people also say after spending about five minutes in his presence and being mesmerized by all he has to offer is this: "Man! I tell you what: he has got to have the hottest girlfriend ever! I bet she looks like Kim Kardashian after a hot shower." Well, they're not all *that* creative when they say it, but you get the point...

But Dick cringes when he hears this, and those eyes droop a little; he even slumps his toned shoulders. Dick hasn't been laid in months and every time another week goes by with no action, he starts to wonder if he got this name in the story as a painful reminder of the thing he'll never actually get to use! But why would this be a problem for Dick, you might ask? It's not as easy as you think; it's not like the movies. Some women flock to Dick because of his car and looks, but how on Earth are they supposed to hang out with the guy if he's petrified to speak to them?

You see, Dick is just plain, old terrified to talk to women. It's not because he's intimidated by them, but he experiences something that a lot of you may experience in one aspect of life or another: *Dick's afraid to fail.* As stupid as it sounds, he's completely comfortable with keeping his mouth shut and wondering, "What if?" Instead of just saying whatever comes to mind and hoping that it works. Dick would rather let Megan Fox walk away from that luxury car thinking that he was uninterested, instead of having to explain to his friends that he couldn't score a date with her because he didn't know what to say and it turned her off completely. And I have news for Dick: he will sit in that incredible car by himself for the rest of his life if he doesn't suck it up, step out of that comfort zone, and become comfortable with failing until it works.

Are you laughing at Dick while you read this? *Why would you be?* There's no difference between you and Dick. Well, maybe you get a lot more play with the ladies or you don't have a problem with messages flooding your inbox from the handsome guys, but I'm willing to bet that there's something in your life that is of a very similar nature. Perhaps you're the type of person that text messages me on a regular basis with their ambition problems and believe me, there's plenty of them. *I see it and it's like I want to shake them!* It's always people who don't have anything going for them, struggling with depression, and then they'll show these spurts of greatness where they're clearly doing a lot of self-reflecting. I'll always get the messages in the middle of the night and out of nowhere: "I'm doing it, man. I just applied to a ton of jobs. I'm going to wake up tomorrow, follow up, and get myself that opportunity I've always dreamt of. I appreciate the extra push you gave me!" Then, I respond in the morning and get the sound of friggin' crickets chirping in the wind in return, coming to find out that they didn't answer any of the employer's phone calls for the third straight time they tried this. I always want to say, "You clearly want to get out of your shell and start working hard, *so why don't you just do it?*" But I understand that's it's not that easy; what they don't understand is that I was once in their shoes myself, and the reason why I stopped giving them advice is because I came to the realization that I can't help them in any way...

If you're this type of person, sorry, but I can't help you either.

You know why?

Because nobody can help you out of this besides yourself, just like every other problem in life.

If you want to change, *you* need to bring that change about. Can't get ambition going? Suck it up and force yourself to make the phone calls until it pays off, then remember how it felt. Can't stop spending your money on little things that don't matter? Force yourself to save your money for two weeks, then buy something nicer than usual and remember how it felt. That feeling of satisfaction will carry you; it will make you realize how many accomplishments you've been missing out on by staying in that comfort zone instead of doing what scares you. And you'll never want to go back to that place where you felt 'comfortable' again when it happens! All it takes is one time to experience the beautiful feeling that embracing change brought you and you'll find yourself in a new comfort zone, one that is a lot easier to sit comfortably in.

You know how I know? Dick isn't a fictional character. I'm Dick, and yes, I totally named myself 'Dick' because that's what I think about my former alter-ego that was terrified to talk to women throughout most of my life. You know how many times I've had a beautiful blonde sitting next to me in a bar, eyeballing me and I spent the next five minutes visualizing all that I wanted to say to her only to watch her walk away and dance up on some meat head instead of me? It's sickening to ponder; I wonder how many amazing relationships I missed out on by being a chicken! I'd show up to family parties answering all these questions about what I was going to accomplish next, shaking hands and smiling while everyone told me 'how proud of me' they were, then I'd drop my head and go silent when they asked where my prize of a girlfriend was. It ate away at me for years and luckily for me, there's plenty of free-spirited women who will go with a guy who can't make conversation to save his life! Sheesh. If there wasn't, I'd probably still be a virgin as we speak!

You know how that changed for me? Exactly how I said it'd change for you guys... I was sitting in a bar in Columbus, Ohio, holding a Red Bull energy drink in my hand because I couldn't drink any alcohol. (Yeah, you know why…) Now looks aren't everything, but there wasn't a whole lot of good-looking women in this place, in my opinion. Besides the one sitting across from me by herself, with the green dress and eyes to match. The dim light in this dirty bar happened to shine on her and it was reminiscent of a movie scene where the question might as well have been written on the wall above her head: "I put it on a platter for you this time, Dick. Are you going to say something? How many more times are we going to go through this…I've been throwing them at you for years, you dick!"

This next part wasn't in my mind, either; it happened just like this: the nine guys who were also dumb enough to go to this bar instead of the other five-hundred beautiful bars in Columbus looked at her, looked at each other, and then stared at me as if they came with the guy who wrote the message above her head. "No, seriously, are you going to talk to her, or do we have to?" The bearded guy next to me, who looked like some twisted version of Tony Soprano who lost his money and got kicked out of the mafia, didn't say it out loud, but that's honestly how it felt…

Then it happened, and I hope it happens for you someday in whatever action you're struggling to take. My dad wasn't there to pressure me into doing it, so I didn't die alone. Tony Soprano next to me didn't give me permission. My friends didn't make me do it. I finally snapped and did it myself! With my leg practically shaking, visualizing the forty-eight different ways that I could trip and fall on the way over there, I dragged my expensive Jordans and my Red Bull next to her, while thinking of ten different lies about why I was drinking that instead of a beer like everyone else. There's no dialogue to follow here; there's no lie about how I swept her off her feet with some slick words that leaked out of my mouth. I was awkward. I was everything that I was terrified of being before. But you know what happened? *I ended up seeing the girl for five months.* This isn't the part of the book where I pretend like my expertise is in dating now, but even though it didn't turn out to be my wife, that was an enormous moment for me where something that had held me back in life would never go on to be a problem again. Amazingly enough, meeting new women has now become one of the more effortless parts of my life. And all because I grew the courage to snap out of it one time!

Can you imagine your own story in this chapter of the book? Which part are you on? Are you ready to tell the happy ending? Or are you going to continue sitting in that comfort zone and feeling sorry for yourself? Dating is one thing, but most things we're afraid of in life are just a figment of our imagination. That barrier, that wall of a comfort zone in our mind tries to tell us that there's some diabolical outcome on the other side of trying to snap out of it, but how could we ever know what'll happen if we don't just suck it up and try for once? I mean, really, why do you think I quoted the people that I did at the beginning of this chapter? To sell some copies of a book? No, not even close. I study sales, remember? A quote isn't going to sell this for me; I mentioned them so that you can stop reading right now, go back and read those again, and then come back to this point in the chapter. What's the one thing each quote had in common? Those highly successful people are telling you that the other side of your comfort zone is where you want to be, and I'm here to tell you that all you need to do to see how beautiful it truly is would be to suck it up, give it a try, and see how incredible you feel. It's like the devil knows what you're capable of; he doesn't want to see how amazing you are at your true potential, so he puts that barrier in your mind to trap you down there on Earth with all the normal people who are also terrified to conquer what they're afraid of. Imagine the look on his face when you grow the courage to erase that one flaw you have. An amazing vision to have, isn't it? Now how about you put forth some effort to turn that vision into a reality…

People like Barrack Obama don't sit in that comfort zone and wonder what's it like to be the first black president; they don't stay at home and become another nameless politician because they're *not* afraid of fear. I don't want you to be afraid of fear, either. The fear of change is not only holding you back from becoming the happiest and richest version of yourself, it's holding you back from achieving *true confidence* in yourself. As you're starting to realize by now, I assume, every chapter in this book is like a puzzle in which you can't unlock the power if you don't have every piece assembled. Once you've given it a shot and conquered that fear, you'll come to find that you have the confidence to believe that you can do *anything.* But without understanding that confidence and how it works, you can fall into the trap of becoming arrogant or even worse, feeling like you've done enough to settle for what you've accomplished already. I could never let that happen to anybody, so let me share with you the best story of what confidence can do for you that I believe the world has ever seen…

This story is about somebody who literally re-wrote what's possible in his profession simply because he believed that he could. Somebody who was once a 'nobody' like the rest of us, yet he went on to become one of the biggest stars in the world when all the signs pointed to him having zero right to be…

Ladies and gentlemen, introducing, fighting out of the red corner... This man is a mixed-martial artist, holding a professional record of twenty-one wins, four loses. Standing at five-foot, nine inches tall, he weighed in at one-hundred and forty-five pounds. Presenting, the pride of Ireland and the reigning, defending, featherweight champion of the world! (Come on, man. It's still his title…)

"The Notorious…"

Conor McGregor.

CHAPTER V:
Confidence: Lefty

"All that matters is how you see yourself."

Conor McGregor, the first man to ever hold titles in two divisions simultaneously in the history of the UFC.

At fifteen-years old with that mop of a haircut and the over-sized, buggy eyes, I sat still in a wooden chair as my stepdad's crooked teeth flew into the room via a lunge to pry my puny frame from the routine video game binge. This drastic action was necessary, due to the fear that I may never leave that room and attempt to socialize on my own. I have got to give it to Charley: despite not being my father or related to me in any way, he really *did* care about me and I know the guy still does! I'm very thankful that he had something to do with my life, especially when it comes to what he did for me that night…

Now that I really think about it, he just wanted to get hammered with his doctor and didn't want my mom to come home to find out that he had left me there alone to throw a raging party again, so he invited me to watch what I called "some UFC fight" at the time, right? Any who, we get to the house and the guy's pad is enormous, as we enter this all-white room filled with leather furniture, an 80-inch flat screen TV showing the fights, and a glass coffee table in the middle that was littered with gourmet snacks and beer. Charley and I were surrounded by four other people who looked like my stepdad AKA dressed like hobos with tattoos. After a mere moment of looking around the room and realizing that the only people in it with a reading level above the third grade were the doctor and I, I turned my head away from the alcohol to pretend that I wasn't craving it and gazed my eyes upon my first Mixed Martial Arts fight...

Something like a black hole sucking in a random planet was the incredible tug the fight had upon my eyes, as I watched Rafael Dos Anjos get knocked unconscious by Jeremy Stephens in what would turn out to be one of the greatest knockouts in the history of the sport. The uppercut gained its force through a running start, which is unheard of in the sport, and the only thing that would hit Dos Anjos harder for the rest of his life was the mat as the back of his head smashed against the ground. And as the energy of the room reached a level that is only comparable to apes in the jungle pounding their chests as they prepared to fight over the last banana, I smiled with wide eyes and decided that I couldn't die without first experiencing the feeling of lacing up the gloves.

I'd proceed to dedicate years upon years of my life to training in the sport and idolizing the men—and eventually women—who participated in it. I can one-hundred percent attest to the fact that it is the single-most difficult thing on Earth to master. Boxers only need to know how to box. Wrestlers only need to know how to wrestle. MMA fighters need to train daily on multiple arts to learn how to defend themselves or they'll be embarrassed by the men/women who can. It'd be like asking a tennis player to suddenly learn how become a professional at baseball and soccer, except that tennis player wouldn't have to worry about getting his teeth kicked in if he couldn't accomplish it. And to be completely honest with you, my body wasn't built for the sport. I spent the last two years battling injuries and backing out of the bouts I agreed to participate in before I'd eventually decide that I was better off sticking to the cardio aspect of it and not taking the damn thing that serious.

...

That was a lie...

My career didn't end because of injuries; injuries were just an excuse I used to hide the fact that I wasn't tough enough to compete against people who weren't afraid to get injured. I could've fought if I wanted to be a fighter, but I didn't because the easy way out was to come up with phony stories about why I couldn't achieve greatness at it. I quit; I became the epitome of wasted talent, as I threw away the natural gift of quick hands. My last day training was when my coach in Cincinnati gave me the task of teaching the terrified new girl how to hold her hands up and throw the basic combinations. Her lip was quivering when I threw fake punches at her; I even let her get a couple shots in to build her confidence. I checked my Facebook a few years later to see her holding up an amateur championship belt for the city of Cincinnati, not to mention living out my dream while I put my beer down and made mental note not to anger this girl if I ever ran into her again.

The day I decided that I 'couldn't do it' is fresh in memory and came long before I officially threw in the towel in my forgettable fighting career. I was at a local MMA show in Youngstown hosted at what was called "The Brawlroom" where people from my local MMA team used to compete in the early stages of their careers. *They were fighting in a damn ring instead of a cage!* That bothered me badly, since it's common knowledge that Mixed Martial Arts is supposed to be inside of a cage to add to the entertainment side of the sport and give it a 'badass, life or death' feel. I slouched in my seat inside of this small and broken-down brick building, wearing a flat-brim hat backwards that read "Streetfighter" while sporting an all-black shirt that had my MMA team's name written in gold lettering. Sitting next to me were two friends from high school, also sitting in steel folding chairs like I was, and their mouths were wide-open in excitement because my teammate was in full-mount on some guy (sitting on his chest) while completely beating the peanuts out of him. Not that they had any reason to cheer for the guy but put alcohol and drugs into the body of sixteen-year old kids and it's not that difficult to get them fired up about anything at all, really. The crowd rose to its feet and joined them in screaming like wild animals, all while I remained slouched and stared *through* the fight, seemingly into space itself...

Look at how low-level this event is, I thought, none of these guys can possibly make it big. *They don't even look that talented.* They have got to see and feel that, right? Am I wasting my time with all of this? Maybe I should treat this as a hobby and take school seriously. I can't ever amount to anything being around this type of thing! My dad has never lost a fight in his life and he said my defense sucks, anyway. So, really, what's the point of being here besides another reason for us to drink?

And here we are years later, as I was at work today before I wrote this and—out of boredom—began scrolling through YouTube videos because I guess my time with this company is coming to an end (I took another job a month after writing that sentence). I came across a video of Conor McGregor and even if I didn't introduce him or strongly hint that he's an MMA fighter with all of this, did you guys really need an introduction of who that is? What first caught my eye was his name, of course, but I was drawn to this video rather than the rest for reasons that I couldn't pinpoint. As I continued to watch, it was obvious to put two and two together and notice that it was one of his very first fights. *I had never seen this one before!* The building hosting the event Conor fought in was *identical* to the one I described myself sitting in almost ten years prior, with the steel chairs and all—like a parallel universe hosting the same event, yet in Ireland. And that was enough to make sure that I'd watch the video the whole way through. Within mere moments, Conor had his opponent mounted in the same way that my teammate had his and he showed mercy, finishing the man quickly instead of taking his life from him. As the small crowd cheered for the man that they didn't know would go on to become one the most well-known celebrities in the world, that same man walked over to the camera with zero emotion as an eruption of noise engulfed him. He stepped over the rope of the ring, put his face into the lens of the camera and pointed at it with his finger, then with wide eyes filled with *confidence*, he proclaimed: "*I am the fucking future.*"

Chills shot up my spine, and a sign above my head that read, "The hair on the back of his neck is standing up" couldn't have made it more obvious to anyone that I was infatuated with what I had just seen. But it wasn't the aura of Conor that got to me; I knew intuition had me paying close attention to the similarities of the event I attended and the one that I was watching for a reason. Same exact type of venue, same low-level of fighting, same small crowd, same no-name teams, yet Conor McGregor walked into that ring with the mindset that he was *already* the future. He strutted in there *knowing* that he was the best in the world, even though the world didn't know his name. I sat in a similar venue and said that nobody surrounding me could possibly be capable of such things, including myself. That difference in confidence is what gave him a shot, and that's the same reason why my MMA career ended before it even began. But confidence didn't just help him in the ring and there's a bigger picture I'd like to paint using Conor's example: this wasn't some gifted individual put into the right circumstances who was lucky enough to be confident in himself, he comes from nothing. *There's no reason that he should be where he is today!*

This man was a plumber at one point. He dropped that plumbing career to pursue his fighting dream and had no income, which isn't the brightest decision regardless of how easily you're winning your first few fights. His wife worked low-end jobs to support them, as Conor picked up $215 unemployment checks and continued taking years off his life training. They were part of a situation that's all too common in our world today, one where a man has a dream and the only person who supports him is his spouse. How would you react if a girl you knew was dating a guy on unemployment that swears that he's the next big thing in the world of martial arts? Most people probably thought it was a joke, but Conor kept pushing. Conor was tuning out everything and everyone around him, saying to himself that he would one day be world champion. And all training aside, those moments and that mindset is *exactly* why people like Conor McGregor will be remembered forever...

Let me remind you that MMA is a sport that people don't want to pursue. Not because of the difficulty, but because it's one of the most un-rewarding professions in the world in terms of the effort that you need to put forth and what the odds say you'll get paid (and that's for a good professional fighter, too). The biggest title fights in the UFC had only yielded a few million dollars in total before Conor got there. And that isn't what the fighters make, that's what *everyone* in the organization makes including the owners. Then you subtract the costs incurred to put together an event like this, you pay for advertising—yikes! Aside from sponsors, only the best in the world could make a million or two a year. And if you think that's a lot, keep in mind that an accountant with a salary of $60,000 will make $2,700,000 in a 45-year career before taxes as MMA fighters can realistically only expect to fight for about eight and the average guy only takes home five figures per fight. (They only fight a few times a year…)

MMA was always a side note to boxing, even to the WWE and the rest of professional wrestling, which is all staged to begin with! There was never a thought that an MMA fighter could even dream of making what a boxer would make…*and then came along the lefty from Ireland.* You all know Conor for his big mouth and ability to market himself while backing it up, but what he accomplished in taking home $100 million fighting Floyd Mayweather is something that was legitimately considered impossible *until he went ahead and did it.* So, let's tie it all together: the same man who sat in venues competing with 'nobodies' while being a 'nobody' himself was able to accomplish something that was considered impossible until he said so. That's the same man who was a plumber, the same man who was once on welfare, and all because he went through that while telling himself, *"I am the fucking future."*

Ladies and gentlemen, my beloved readers, the power of having confidence in yourself is what gives you a fighting chance. The only person who will ever be able to tell you that you can't do something is yourself. The only person who decides whether tomorrow can be the most productive day of your entire life or not is yourself. The only person who decides whether you can get clean or not is yourself. Rehab can only do so much; I can only say so much! *You need to develop that confidence to fight for a better day on your own.* And know that there is no benefit in attempting to develop confidence over an extended period. The longer it takes, the less of a chance you have to develop it. *You simply decide that you are capable right now.*

Don't read that and shake your head either; it's real. You just need to say it, scream it, believe in it. And if you don't believe me, I want you to look up some of Conor's rants or fights and analyze the look in his eyes while he's scripting this amazing story of his. I want you to look at his life with all that luxury, all that fame, and that incredible legacy he accomplished before 30-years old, and then I want you to sit and ponder on the story I just told you about how I sat in a venue just like his telling myself that type of journey isn't possible. Look at the difference in his life and ours, do you see what confidence can do for you? People like Conor prove that nothing is impossible, so stop convincing yourself that it is.

But, as always, there's more to this story, just as there is to every story. I'd like to spend the next chapter answering another one of those infinite questions that might be floating around in your brain as you read this, which may be, "How on Earth is it possible to maintain a level of confidence that I've never had before? Won't there be hard days, Danny? What if I have a moment where I lose my new-found confidence, then how the hell will I continue with my Process?"

You use something else that Conor uses, that I use, that every celebrity uses, that every president uses, and that anybody who has ever accomplished anything important uses. It's something that I call your "dream-triggers."

Another one of those buttons you press in the bad times and it will instantly drag you back into that realm where you have infinite confidence and the heart of the most ferocious lion in the jungle...

It's the art of visualization.

CHAPTER VI:

Dream Triggers: You Have to Visualize

"Act as if you're a wealthy man, rich already, and then you'll surely become rich. Act as if you have unmatched confidence and then people will surely have confidence in you. Act as if you have unmatched experience and then people will follow your advice. And act as if you are already a tremendous success, and as sure as I stand here today – you will become successful."

Jordan Belfort, *The Wolf of Wall Street.*

I WAS SITTING at a long black desk in Langsam library at UC with my breath reeking of cigarettes and Adderall leaking from my nose, as my head tilted upwards and to the left where I would begin to space out. The unfashionable glasses on my head were being pressed so hard behind my ears that it began to cause a throbbing pain down through my neck; the feeling caused me to shift my focus away from the incredible-looking, wooden architecture that was the second floor of the library. This feeling was reminiscent of the one I had when I first experienced an overdose and I think we can all understand why I wouldn't want to dwell on it at the time. That brings me to this next piece said to me by a close friend who was studying with me, "Have you seen that new movie yet? You know, the one about the crazy rich dude doing all the drugs? It made me think of you when I watched it!" Nice, Danny, real nice… "Thanks for staring into fucking space while we were supposed to be studying, by the way!"

"Piss off." I said, as I sniffled and wiped my nose after a quick twitch. "I need to quit hitting Addy before I participate in literally every event life has to offer."

"Isn't that shit supposed to make you focus?" My friend asked. The words were coming out of his bald head so slow that I thought my own brain had *finally* stopped functioning properly. "Have you ever sat and thought about the fact that it has the opposite effect on you, so you probably shouldn't be snorting it, what, fourteen times a day?"

"Fuck off," I snapped, but only after another sniffle (of course). "Wait, what movie?"

"*The Wolf of Wall Street.*" He returned, while rubbing his gut. He said this next sentence while flinging his fingers into the air like an artist outlining his next great portrait, but the kid didn't have a creative bone in his body. "It's like our generation's *Blow*. Since you're going to flunk your next drug test at work and be homeless as a result, you might as well stay here and watch it! Get nice and cozy, bud!"

Vin Diesel Head, as we'll call him, would proceed to walk out the revolving glass doors at the front of the library where he would enter our beautiful campus, which was littered by little gleams of light from the sunshine outside. The group of kids strutting in front of the library were all smiling, likely talking about how nice it was to be outside, also how thankful they were to have apartments that weren't filled with roaches like I did! Any who, that thought of the roaches waiting for me under my bed—the only article of furniture in the place—kept me from rushing home any time soon. I started to think of any excuse not to study for the test I would ultimately fail and instead, began preparing the speech to my professor about letting me pass anyway, as always. Something inside of me kept tugging my attention towards the movie Vin Diesel Head had mentioned, though. Crazy to think back on it now, but the only way to put it is that it had triggered my intuition to the point of where I felt like I *had to* watch it...

The opening scene started with Leonardo Dicaprio playing this businessman I had never heard of, then one of the first things to come out of his mouth is that 'he,' Jordan Belfort, uses something along the lines of twenty drugs a day. My first thought was: ok, clearly exaggerated since the guy watching the movie uses about four a day and even that number had my doctor mind-blown to the point of instructing his intern to do a research paper on me for his grad school final. Next, it's mentioned that the same man also earned *forty-nine million dollars in one year* while in his mid-twenties. *Whoa.* Kids in the library would come and go for the next three hours, studying and socializing in whispers, some would even walk past me, but I saw none of them. The lines between my peripheral vision blurred to the point of where a tornado could've blasted through the library and it would've lifted me from my seat, yet I wouldn't have blinked. I would've only tried to take my computer with me to continue watching this spectacle before my eyes.

There are many scenes that were memorable in this masterpiece directed by the legend, Martin Scorcese, but the moment that would stick with me was the scene where Belfort was standing in front of the hundreds of employees working for him at the office he founded. He takes center stage in front of the audience and even has a microphone, then gives the most incredible motivational speech you'll ever hear in your life. The crowd is roaring, as he screams with fire in his eyes that they need to pick up the phone and sell his company's new stock or die trying. Even though it was a staged scenario, adrenaline flowed throughout my body and out of my fingertips as I gripped the computer, sat up in my seat, and began to see exactly what I wanted to be someday. It was the first time I knew what I wanted my occupation to be, and what I wanted people to see when they looked at me: *Mr. Success.* The man they took advice from, not the man taking that advice…

I laugh now at how insane I truly was at a younger age, but now I sit here and thank Jordan Belfort for what that day did to me. I obsessed over his life and who he was, not in the sense of wanting to be him but wanting to know what steps he took to become *they* man. How he acted, how he spoke, what type of women he was around, what type of drugs he used, his quotes, his education—*I wanted to know everything.* I knew that if I put my focus on that man and took similar steps to the ones taken in his shoes that I'd have a chance to become the man in that movie. I watched that scene hundreds of times over the course of the next few months, and that led to me digging into what really happened in real life. Belfort's memoir, *The Wolf of Wall Street*, which the film was based upon, says it went differently. It doesn't mention the intensity and the real quotes used were quite different (you know Hollywood has got to exaggerate it to get their money. I don't blame them!). The closing statement of the chapter, the real-life scenario, held that quote I referred to at the beginning of this chapter. Once I read it, it clicked to me: *that's how he got there.* That's how he became the man that I wished I was at the time and the person I worked every day to become. Not the drugs, not the fraudulent sales tactics, or the prostitutes, or the swearing, or the charisma, or any of the stupid, wild things the man did in his insane life...I'm talking about the secret he let out when he gave that advice to that room full of ambitious people who dreamt of being 'the man...'

He told them to visualize.

In that moment, Belfort's employees weren't where they wanted to be in life. They were successful, but they wanted big-time millions like Jordan had and he told them, if they wanted to get there, that they needed to walk around with their chest puffed out *acting like they were there already.* It's even more so about picturing it in your head than it is about confidence. It made me think back to how Jordan's story started and that's with him and a few idiots in a garage using cheap telephones to sell penny stocks, yet they ended up becoming some of the richest people in the history of Wall Street. Jordan's lunatic salesman became millionaires because they were constantly working towards that picture he painted in their minds: the one where they were *already* rich, even though they *weren't* close in real life! Then, soon enough, that cheap garage became an incredible office where people flooded the entrance to throw their resumes at the secretaries in hopes to work for the firm, as those people who used to dream of being millionaires sat in that office *currently worth millions.*

I was a broke, underachieving drug addict that wanted to be an author, businessman, and public speaker like Jordan Belfort. I kept that quote in mind when I went to the grocery store and couldn't afford groceries, eating chicken pot pies and ramen noodles like a bum while high on drugs and depressed. I used to walk through those aisles and imagine myself walking through the store with a happier look on my face, wearing a golden watch with a Ralph Lauren suit on my back. I'd grab those groceries, walk to my car, and see that horrendous-looking Toyota Camry; I'd grit my teeth each time! *I couldn't even look women in the eyes while getting into that car.* A mega car wash funded by Warren Buffet himself couldn't do damage to the black smudges on that thing. But you know what I did when I got into the car? I'd *visualize* myself driving a tinted-out BMW with custom rims and then I'd head home and keep that picture in mind throughout the drive's duration. I'd channel all that rage and use it to study, even when I didn't want to; I wanted success so bad that it would force my body to do things. That visualization in my mind promised me that one day it would all be worth it...

Looking back on it now, I'm in this position at twenty-six years old because of the picture that movie created in my head. Now I picture having a Maserati in my possession by thirty-five years old and a life filled with so much money that my future children will never have to worry about a thing. They won't have to go through life focusing on money because it's nothing to them; they'll have always had it. And I want you to thoroughly analyze the previous passage, also to think about Jordan's rise to power and how that affected my life in a positive way, then I want you to paint a picture of where you can be in the next few years if you work hard enough. *Obsess* over it like he did. *Obsess* over it like I did. Ask yourself, where do you want to be in five years? How about ten? On a smaller scale, who do you want to be tomorrow? Do you wish you could wake up tomorrow and be free from depression? Then picture it now before you read any further. Come to a complete stop, close your eyes, and *dream* about who you want to be. That dream-trigger is going to end up being the anecdote to your low confidence days. If you want to be that person bad enough, then that image will force you to keep going.

Motivation is such a problem for most people; doubt floods their mind and makes them think that they're supposed to be a certain way, or that they're only destined for a certain amount of success, or that they're doomed for failure in general. But those people fail to realize that none of the above is even close to being true. You *create* your future by the effort you put forth daily and by building on that confidence in bulk as you go. When you find yourself in a situation like I was in inside of that grocery store, you need to let your mind drift and focus on that picture you just painted from the questions I asked above. Ask it to anybody that knows me: *I'm an airhead!* I'm constantly playing with the skin on my face while seemingly staring at nothing, but I don't even realize how strange I look because I'm that deep in thought. I had a friend count that I once did it one-hundred times while in his presence in a single day. And I didn't tell him, but I'm telling you that this type of visualizing is what's going through my mind when my thoughts seem to have separated me from reality. I'm always visualizing to keep that hunger there, and to keep me focused on where I want to be, so that I can make sure I arrive at that destination as fast as possible. If you want to accomplish something that you consider difficult to attain, then you have got to be willing to be an airhead! Stop caring about how you look to others; your goal should be a lot bigger than their opinion of you when you zone into your dream triggers. Do it as often as you must to make that picture feel realistic, then capitalize from the confidence of how real that picture feels and work towards that feeling…

Be cautious though, as this practice can swing your future the other way if it's not used correctly. I want you to think of where you are in life and I don't care if you're a fifteen-year old kid or a thirty-year old druggie…you're in that place because that's what you visualized, that's what you believed you were meant to be. The fifteen-year old that lacks direction was born without it, so he went through his first fifteen years accepting the fact that he had no guidance and began to visualize a life without guidance. Now he's fifteen-years old and still walks the Earth without guidance; he won't ever have direction until the day that he begins to visualize that he can figure out everything in life by himself. If he's smart, he'll live the rest of his days working hard at that picture he painted in his head until one day he's giving guidance to others. That thirty-year old druggie? He began to use drugs and visualized a life where he couldn't separate himself from them, so he got worse and worse until the point of where he was an addict. Now that negative visualization grew into one where he would lose his job and end up in rehab, so rehab and being broke is ultimately where he finds himself. What if he had painted a picture where he walked into the trap house, changed his mind about purchasing the poison, and walked out to go turn his life around? What if he believed in that vision and walked into that same trap house with a great attitude that day, living out his fantasy and thus living an entirely different life? Where would he be today?

Age has nothing to do with how this works; your visualization becomes real as soon as you put in the necessary work to make it so. I know a seventeen-year old kid who's richer than 99.9% of the people reading this. I call him T-Planes and he drives a nice Porsche around that he paid for himself off an online internet business, the same one he used to visualize driving while people doubted that his ideas would work. *60K followers and counting on the kid's Instagram page!* That fact and the paragraphs above should really put this next statement into perspective for you: it's not you are, it's not how you're raised, it's not where you're from, *it's the picture you paint of yourself and where you believe that you're headed.* It's your attitude towards every single situation you walk into in life and how you visualize those various situations going. You can handle any situation in life so long as you see a great outcome and you work towards that great outcome until it happens with zero doubt in your mind that it may not. Amazing to think that another perfect example played on my headphones as I was typing this, like it was just meant to be! And for that, I simply can't leave it out. Logic, the hip hop artist and one of the best the world will ever see, just rapped the following lyrics on the song *44 Bars*: "I used to think the fame and money was the motivation, until I toured the world and met the people face to face and understood that the power was harnessed in that basement..."

This is referring to something Logic talks about a lot, which was how he began his entire legacy in his friend's basement with the world doubting that he had a chance to become a household name. Let's now dig into the song *Take it Back* where Logic spits the following, while ranting at the end in third person: "Now I want you to also imagine, that, at seventeen-years old, this child, okay, leaves home and gets two jobs to support himself. Two jobs that he works in the morning and the evenings and then he would come home to about eight or nine hours of sleep. But spend four, five, six hours of that working on music. Persevering, grabbing the remote control and *looking in the mirror and pretending to see thousands and thousands and thousands of people just chanting his name.* Hoping that it would happen."

And now when Logic travels the world and gets on stage, he grabs a real microphone and thousands of people *do* scream his name, all because he visualized that picture in that basement. A belief in yourself, a clear picture painted in your head and constantly thought about is powerful, guys. *Embrace it.* But to completely honest with you, visualization is a small sliver of something much greater. Something that some people think is made-up or some type of voodoo, but it is, in fact, the closest thing to *real* magic that life has. This superpower is something that not only controls the events of your life, but who comes into your life, what kind of weather on what days, what kind of traffic you're driving into, what kind of job you get, the mood of the guy interviewing you, and so on. Part of me wanted to write that I wished I had found it sooner in life, but the other part of me laughed because I now understand how it works. This power found me at the perfect time, just like it was supposed to. And exactly when it was supposed to, just like everything else in my life, since, of course, that is the type of control that it has.

You know, some people that see me on my good days ask me, "What's your secret?"

Then, I hide nothing and give them just what they're asking for, except they chuckle or think that I'm kidding!

"Uh, my secret is *The Secret...*"

Have you ever heard of the Law of Attraction?

CHAPTER VII:

What Goes Around, Comes Around: The Law of Attraction

"We become what we think about. Energy flows where attention goes."

Rhonda Byrne, author of *The Secret*.

WHAT ARE YOU doing?

"Reading your book..."

No, no, no... I mean, what *exactly* are you doing? You're probably sitting in a chair, or laying in your bed, or maybe you're even standing in the kitchen doing something I can't stand, which is reading eleven pages of a book before work. *You know, as if that will benefit you in some way!* How on Earth can your mind process a message if you're only taking in a tiny percentage of that message at a time? Sheesh, develop some time management. Don't read it until you have a few hours of free time, so that you can really apply yourself and let it sink in. Anyway, regardless of whether you're sitting or standing, you're not floating in circles or towards the nearest cloud in the sky, correct? So, why aren't you floating?

"Uh, gravity?"

Yes, gravity! That thing that you can't remember learning about in grade school that is so widely accepted as something you 'just know' that you consider it to be 100% factual. When somebody brings this fact up to you, you may even have a lightbulb go off in your head that tells you there's something called the 'law of gravity.' Did you know that it's not a fact? It's just a theory. Think about it: can you *physically* see gravity? Or you do you just accept that it's real because Isaac Newton is one of the smartest people to ever live and 'proved' to the world that it *must* be real? Newton thought that something like gravity *must* exist because a friggin' apple fell off a tree and onto his head; what else could've pulled that apple downward towards his dome? (Story goes that it fell from a tree near him and not onto his head, but the first story is the one we'll stick with as it sounds much better!) He went on to do a ridiculous amount of research to put together this theory of its existence, something that even Einstein would go on to research further in his own 'Theory of Relativity' to tie this thought into how the planets move the way that they do. The only reason it's so widely accepted is that they provided 'proof' that there's such a strong gravitational pull in the universe that if there *weren't* something like gravity, then we'd all just be floating around in circles. But we can't officially see proof of this, so how do we know it exists? We don't. It's considered a fact because it has *got to be* a fact, or the way things work won't make sense!

So, when I begin to tell you about the Law of Attraction I want you to understand that this is not some ridiculous idea created by a wonderful woman named Rhonda Byrne that I was crazy enough to accept as factual because I'm just plain crazy in general. If you believe in the law or theory of gravity because it's what you were taught, yet you'll read what I'm about to tell you about the Law of Attraction and you don't believe that it's real, then you're completely naïve to the fact that you're being hypocritical! To believe in the Law of Attraction once you come to understand it would be no different than believing in the law or theory of gravity, as more highly intelligent people than you'd ever believe confirm that they know about its existence, whether they reference it directly or not. You see, Rhonda's book *The Secret* was published in 2006, but the information it holds goes way back to before even Jesus Christ himself was walking around the Earth and turning water into wine. The book is a manual on how to use the Law of Attraction, but even more so the evidence that proves that people have been using this law without realizing it for as long as time has ticked. There are quotes confirming this, ranging from Tesla to age-old philosophers and even countless doctors of today, along with lawyers and other people who are doing incredibly well for themselves. It's the power of positivity and how you can use it to attract what you want to come into your life…

Anything you want.

The law states that whatever you give out to the universe through your thoughts, words, and actions, you must receive in return. This ranges from something as small as yelling, "Fuck!" as you spill your coffee on your lap to wishing the guy sitting next to you would lose his job. Some people read something like that and don't dive deep enough into the thought, as they'll swear out loud, look around and see that nothing out of the ordinary happened, then laugh about the fact that they almost believed it. They may even proceed to go on with their lives telling people about how big of an idiot Danny Range is! Ah, but then the next day, or maybe the next hour, they're driving down the road and the guy in front of them throws a cigarette out of his window, which lands in their lap and they yell "Fuck!" out loud. And they'll do so without thinking twice about the fact that they yelled that same quote out loud yesterday, so they attracted a reason to have to yell it out loud again…

Now I bet some of you are shaking your head, but stop and think about it: when is the last time something bad happened in your life? Maybe your spouse cheated on you and you said to yourself, "But I never cheated on them!" I'm here to point out to you that you either consistently thought about the fact that they may be cheating on you and you attracted it to yourself or you made fun of somebody who was once cheated on and you attracted it in that way. The way the law works is deep enough to point of where you could've even wished the worst thing to happen to somebody else, so you attracted the worst thing to happen to yourself, which was to be cheated on. If your life isn't going the way that you want it to, you likely haven't been aware of your thoughts consistently because nobody ever stressed to you how important it is to do so. Now that you have had somebody open your mind to this, you can begin to pay attention to it, see its effect, and start to understand just how much of your life you've massacred by simply feeling bad about things or giving your energy to negativity. You can get your mind right and start to see everything turn around for you or continue to let negativity infect you; it's your choice, so why not choose to be open-minded and experience more positive outcomes in life?

Listen, it's everywhere.

It's everything you do, everything you say, everything you think, and most importantly, it's how you feel. *You need to feel good.* If you don't feel good, you're instantly attracting negative thoughts and negative things to come into your life. If you truly believe everything in life is a coincidence, then you'll attract a life of coincidence where everything happens by chance; why leave it to chance when you can imagine a life that always goes well?

Not only do I highly encourage you to get a greater understanding of this by buying *The Secret* and digging into it yourself, but I also encourage you to give thought to the elementary summary I just shared with you before you do so. Before I move onto my own example, I want to use a perfect example from your own life. At the end of the day today or if you're currently at the end of the day, I want you to put this book down upon finishing this paragraph and give serious thought to these following questions for a moment: How did your day go? Good or bad, obviously, but *why* did it go good or bad? If it went well, you likely woke up in a good mood, believed that the day would go well, and walked around knowing that it was a good day, right? If it went terribly, did you feel bad when you woke up? Oh, no? Then something clearly happened to make your day go bad, so did you consider it a possibility that the bad event could occur at one point? Maybe not today, but at one point in time you accepted that it was possible that you didn't get that job or that you'd still be fat today or that you'd still be broke, right? So, you could *feel* that there was a possibility of the bad event occurring, it came to you because you *believed* it could happen, and then how did you react afterward? You felt like crap, didn't you? And the rest of that day went terrible, didn't it? *Yeah, I bet it did!* Wait, it didn't? So, you felt as if your fortunes would turn around and then you felt good about your chances of a good day, so you believed in that thought and ended the day on a good note, didn't you?

Incredible, isn't it? That's why I'm able to write something like that and not think twice about whether you could answer those questions in a different way than I assumed you would. *It's real.* Every moment of your life is created by *you* through the Law of Attraction and if it isn't, it's because you *believe* the Law of Attraction doesn't work, so you're attracting the fact that positivity can't have a positive impact on your life! It makes the hairs raise up on my arms to think about it, and not just the spooky aspect of there being some sort of higher power that controls this, *but it makes me imagine what's possible with such a power.* If you can alter who you are, if you can alter the outcome of every situation in life and in the future, then just *imagine* what you can become…

If you want to attain anything in life, anything at all, ask the universe for it. Say, "I want to get clean of drugs and alcohol." Then, you believe that you have achieved your goal already and while that's the hardest part, it's the most important. It's just like Jordan Belfort said in the chapter covering visualization, remember? Act as if you're rich already, and sure enough, you'll become rich. Do you think Jordan realizes that he used the Law of Attraction to become a millionaire? Finally, the last step is my favorite: after you ask the universe for what you want, you work for it, you believe you already have it *while* you work for it, and you stay feeling good while you work for it, then you get it! It doesn't matter when it gets there; it doesn't matter whether it takes ten years or ten minutes because the universe will deliver it to you when it's meant to happen…

Have you ever heard of the musical artist Russ? He's new, but incredibly talented and he'll be around Hip Hop/R&B for a long time. He tweeted a picture awhile back, one of four books he used to read when he was poor and attempting to make a life for himself through his music. One of the books he swore by was *The Secret*. It's in his lyrics if you listen closely! From his song *Emergency*: "Some people shine and give it back, but my shine is not a lease. This is permanently owned. If I lose it, it's on my terms. I don't wish for shit, *I desire then acquire*." How about the most blatant claim of them all from my favorite song of his? *Just look at the name of the song!* From the song *Manifest*: "Movin' to the rhythm of my intuition. *Anything I want I speak into existence.* That's how I'm living. *That's how I'm winning.*" Russ isn't a good enough example for you? Ok, here's a list of celebrities that have made references to using the various practices that are a part of the Law of Attraction and their exact quotes, which are very easy to find using Google or any search engine:

"Total believer. I believe in manifestation. I believe in putting a rocket of desire out in the universe. *You get it when you believe you have it.* People still sit around and go, 'When it's gonna' come? When it's gonna' come?' And that's the wrong way. You're facing away from it. You have to go, 'It's here! It's here! It's here!'" – Jim Carrey, one of the most recognizable actors in the world. Did you know that Jim Carrey used to drive around the streets of Los Angeles and visualize himself being a famous actor before anybody knew who he was?

"Our thoughts, our feelings, our dreams, our ideas are physical in the universe. That if we dream something, if we picture something, it adds a physical thrust towards realization that *we can put into the universe.*" – Will Smith, also one of the most recognizable actors in the world.

"When I was very young, I visualized myself being and having what it was I wanted. Mentally I never had any doubts about it. The mind is really so incredible. Before I won my first Mr. Universe title, I walked around the tournament like I owned it. *The title was already mine.* I had won it so many times in my mind that there was no doubt I would win it. Then, when I moved on to the movies, the same thing. I visualized myself being a famous actor and earning big money. I could feel and taste success. *I just knew it would all happen.*" – Arnold Schwarzenegger, the friggin' Terminator!

"It happened around five years ago but it's sort of like a mantra. You repeat it to yourself every day. 'Music is my life. Music is my life. *The fame is inside of me.* I'm going to make a number one record and the number one hit.' *And it's not yet, it's a lie.* You're saying a lie over and over and over again. But then one day, *the lie is true.*" – Stefani Joanne Angelina Germanotta AKA 'Lady Gaga,' the singer.

"Like attracts like. *You have to understand you are a magnet.* Whatever you are, that's what you draw to you. If you're negative, you're going to draw negativity. You positive? You draw positive. You're a kind person? Most people are kind to you. *If you see it in your mind, you can hold it in your hand.* This is so true." – Steve Harvey, television host, producer, and proud Cleveland sports fan!

And the list could go on for days…

Open your eyes, guys. Those winners win, and they win because they use the Law of Attraction. You know how the Law of Attraction fell into my hands? I was a few months into being clean and had just started my Instagram account, yet there was immense potential streaming from it. So many people swarmed to my account and I couldn't believe what was happening, as it yielded over six thousand followers in *eight weeks.* A buddy of mine from Youngstown, Frank, loved the content and one day messaged me to ask if I had ever heard of *The Secret.* He said my posts "reminded him of it." I told him no and thought nothing of his recommendation to buy it, until my mother happened to call me within one-hundred seconds of my reply to him, kid you not. My mother, God love her, is big into religion but is by no means someone who thrives off positivity. I tell you this not to belittle her, but to get you to understand how eerie her point in calling me would turn out to be. After asking how I was and telling me about her day, she told me that she had used the end of her check to buy me a few things. She knew I didn't read books at the time but swore that she "felt like I needed to read this one." She said she bought the audible CDs for the car, the DVD, and the book, then said the name of the entire set was *The Secret.*

It blew my mind, and even though I hadn't considered reading it anytime soon, I was a man who understood that you should probably take a sign from above when it's sent to you. Seriously, what are the odds that one person I barely knew too much about and my mother, who knew I didn't like to read, would recommend the same work of art at nearly the same time and not just this, but that they would do so during my first few weeks of being a positive person? Something a lot of people don't know is that, hilariously enough, I was the worst pessimist in the world before all the motivational speaking came about! I assumed the worst would always happen, believed the worst would always happen, and my entire life was filled with all the worst events seemingly being tossed in my direction. People would always laugh when terrible things happened to me, as I had consistently pointed out to them that these things would happen due to my being the "unluckiest guy alive." I never put two and two together that I was attracting that to myself, but there I was, feeling positive for the first time and the Bible of Positivity falls into my lap…

I was hooked, as I become with everything in life because I have an addictive personality, but positivity became the most fascinating addiction I had ever given in to. I had read half the book but was still at the point where most people are when they're introduced to it, which is that it's a fun idea to entertain, but likely isn't entirely real or true. I found myself coming up with various excuses and situations in life where I had been positive yet didn't have a positive outcome and began to become extremely hesitant to fully accept the concept. That is, until the day that I came across the chapter that threw that all out of the window. It's the chapter that made me feel like the book was made entirely for the soul reason of speaking directly to Danny Range. I won't quote it here, but it told me about the necessity of testing out the Law of Attraction using small events instead of bigger ones. I believed landing a movie deal about my life was this enormous, nearly unattainable feat that would make me ball my eyes out if I ever achieved it, one that would make me immortal for achieving, and one that would take decades to accomplish. But the book claimed that was way too big of a fish to catch for my first time in utilizing the Law!

I spent what was likely days and weeks, but only God knows how truly long it took to think of a way to try this out. And then I thought of it: *Traffic.* My pet-peeve! Holy God! *I hate traffic!* Every day though! Every damn day in Columbus there is traffic to the point of where my gym is across the street and two minutes up the road from my day job, yet it takes me twenty minutes to get there. And the morning is much worse. Just imagine Mr. Positivity screaming hysterically at 7 AM because he came to the stop sign at the end of the cul-de-sac and was somehow taken back that the same line of cars had been there that was there the day before, and the day before that, and the day before that. I used to lay awake at night convinced that the people in the cars were spying on me and knew when I'd get to the stop sign, all so that they could plan to be there every morning to see if they could finally make me flip out so bad that I'd drive my car off a bridge. (My paranoia mostly left with the drug use, so that was a wee bit of an exaggeration. But you get the message, I assume...)

So, I tried it. I woke up feeling like garbage for no reason other than the fact that it was 6 AM on a Monday morning, then started my normal routine while visualizing a clear path at the stop sign on my way there. When I got there, what do you think I saw? A clear path like Moses himself parted the red sea in front of me? Nope, I saw my fist flying in front of my face, due to being in the act of punching my steering wheel while screaming bloody murder as I stared at a line of cars that seemed to extend to the border of Mexico. *This was the deepest traffic line of all!* You'd think nine people had died at the intersection, but there was no accident or anything! Not even so much as a dead ant in the damn road, just people forgetting how to drive, per usual. I got to work ten minutes late while shaking my head and thinking that the Law of Attraction wasn't the answer, but then I realized it during the always fun Excel reporting: wait a second, I thought, I woke up feeling like shit, didn't I? If this stuff really works, then that line of cars was there because I felt terrible. And even though I started to visualize the line of cars being gone, it was still there because I felt horrible about being up early on a Monday. *Man!*

I decided to give it one more good try…

Tuesday morning now, as I rose from bed feeling like I had just woken up next to Gigi Hadid (leave me and my fantasies alone). I thought about how amazing my life was now being clean and as I sat in the shower before I left for work, I visualized the cars in that treacherous Mexico traffic line floating forty feet in the air, which allowed me to take the easy left turn while I whistled my way to work with a bright smile! I also began visualizing Route 270 being free of traffic but decided that's too unrealistic to manifest because of the size of the city of Columbus. Yet still, picturing a clear turn out of that cul-de-sac felt so incredible that it made me grin wider than I did in the initial image from my visualization, as I drifted away from reality in the shower. I got out of that shower, got dressed, blasted the music in my car out of appreciation for a happy morning, and got to the stop sign where there was not a single car in sight...

Hold on, I thought, what on Earth just happened?!

Now, admittedly, my previous book told you guys a lot of stories that were exaggerated to make you laugh or prove a point, but I swear on my grandfather's grave that there was not a single car waiting in line for me that day! I'd like you to imagine driving by a stop sign and turning your head when you hear a loud honk only to see the car it came from holding a guy who is seemingly crying tears of joy with his arm sticking out the window in the freezing cold. "He's so happy, what the hell happened to him? I want some of what that guy is smoking!" Nah, you don't, but next I promise that I took a right out of the cul-de-sac, instead of taking a left, just so that I could go in a circle and come back to that stop sign. Part of me still believed I'd come back to see the Mexico line with Gigi Hadid's luxury vehicle leading the charge, as she pointed and laughed and told me that I was still dreaming. I lived at that house for another year, yet never came to be stopped by traffic at that stop sign again. *Not one time though!*

Game, set, match. Danny was sold! I became a full believer and started to research more, thinking to myself, was it impossible for Route 270 to be clear as well? Or was that only impossible for me because I believed in it as a sure fact? Of course, there will always be traffic on 270! Columbus is one of the biggest cities in the US, for God's sake. But one week later I did find a slight left I could take that still led to work and you'd never catch me caught in that horrific traffic jam again. I've embedded this principle into my brain to the point of where I applied it to my ideas before I wrote this chapter; that traffic scenario happened two years ago. Now that I know its power, I know to never write when my mind is on a bad wavelength! Even if I feel like I need to, I make myself watch Dave Chappelle/Kevin Hart standup routines or the final three minutes of the Cavs game seven championship win before I do, so that I'll feel pure happiness before I touch the pad to pen…

Even my first speaking gig came about because of the Law of Attraction. I envisioned myself walking into the California Palms Addiction Treatment Center and landing that opportunity, despite not knowing one person inside or having any sort of appointment with the CEO. I had no speech planned, no sales pitch; the only thing I carried inside was an amazing attitude and a belief in the Law of Attraction. Sebastian, the CEO, just so happened to be taking his first lunch break that month at the same moment, gave me a tour, and informed me that he had just recently considered scheduling their next speaker. Danny Range was booked for October 2017 on the spot! And I can still picture my fingers slapping the keys as I laughed, thinking that the type of BMW I was searching for on the computer was way too personalized to come up for the price that I wanted. But then I paused for a moment and dug into that vision of what I'd look like driving inside it, then I felt as if I had it already, and hit the search button to see my future E90 come up for the price that I wanted. Even though I got rid of the car to save money (maintenance money was not worth looking cool), it was still a dream come true while it lasted! Once you learn how to harness the Law's power, it becomes almost as addicting as experiencing success through your Process when chasing your dreams.

Just remember that there is no such thing as destiny, in my opinion. You're not meant to be anywhere, you're not meant to become anything. That is, of course, unless you create your own destiny by carrying with you the positive vision of what your future will be like. When you're struggling to continue pushing towards change in your life by sticking to your Process, visualize how easy it will be to get used to, then head into the next day of that routine believing that it's *already* easy, and you'll notice that the Law of Attraction will soon make it so. When you're lacking in the discipline department, visualize yourself living a life with no cigarettes or sugary foods or whatever it may be, then head into the next day as if you *already* have that discipline, and soon enough, the Law of Attraction will make you a disciplined person. Use the Law as a crutch, an extra attribute while you're attempting to utilize the rest of the life advice that I've given you. Not only will you notice how much easier this all gets, but you'll notice you're happier overall, which is more important than anything else anyway!

Know that it's nearly impossible to feel happy all the time, so don't feel like you're failing when you read this chapter and don't end up feeling as happy as you believed you would. The Law takes its time, so give it the time that it demands; it will make happiness that much sweeter when it finally arrives. Something Rhonda recommends trying is to aim to be happy fifty-one percent of the time or more, as that officially makes you happy more often than you are negative. And you'll be forced to attract more things to be happy about than to be depressed about!

Although, I like to simplify the way she said it…

I call this process of attempting to master the Law of Attraction…

'Controlling your waves.'

CHAPTER VIII:

Control Your Waves: Master Your Mind, Master Your Life

"Worrying is like praying for something you don't want to happen."

Robert Downey Jr, the Ironman and an advocate of sobriety.

A WHILE BACK, I found myself sitting in my Ohio State shorts that I wear way too much for a guy who didn't attend Ohio State University, while sporting a five-o'clock shadow and a wife beater as I sat on my couch watching the Cavs beat the Nuggets (guess what shorts I'm wearing right now?). And for anybody that has asked me about my writing routines, they'd understand how unusual this is! If I'm 'writing and watching the game,' I'm not watching the game at all. What goes on around me on the usual writing night is a blur; I'll get so sucked into doing what I'm passionate about that the writing begins to flow, as everything else going on in the world becomes meaningless noise falling upon my deaf ears. What made that normal night unique though, was that I was suffering from writer's block. It's only happened two or three times ever, I swear to God! My confidence was crumbling during those days and it took physical force to tilt that chin up, the same one that usually takes twice the effort to tug a centimeter down. OCD kicked in and I felt like everything must be out of order if the usual setting wasn't working. I decided everything around me needed to change and so, I stood up, turned the TV off, went into the bathroom, shaved, then changed my clothes and came back out.

...

Still nothing.

Dumbfounded! Better yet, infuriated and kind of depressed. What, I thought, did I forget how to write? I turned on YouTube and began passing the time while diving into more negative thoughts that the King of Positivity had once forgotten how to experience. That's when I clicked on a random video suggested for me, which seemed odd, as it was nowhere near new or relevant. This interview with the rappers Lil Yatchy and Joe Budden shouldn't have had my interest at all. No disrespect to Yatchy, just not a fan. Budden? Huge fan! Just not of his feisty interviews...

Why were my eyes drawn to this? Intuition again kicking in; I had to watch it, something that made me feel like I'd be shot to death if I didn't. Why though? I should be writing. What other excuse did I have to be sitting in my house by myself on a Friday night? Maybe something in this video has to do with my writing, but how is that even possible? Am I overthinking all of this? Should I just turn the damn Cavs game back on? Well, probably. If J.R. Smith keeps making stupid plays on both sides of the ball, then LeBron is sure to leave again. I better enjoy all this winning while it lasts! (Guess who made a dumb play in The Finals and forced LeBron to leave shortly after I wrote this?) I slugged my coffee with extra caffeine and four espresso shots that practically creates the same feeling as cocaine, and somehow found the audacity to ignore the fact that it could count as a drug relapse with an intelligent enough argument. Then I hit the play button…

Two minutes in and these two genuinely get into an intelligent conversation that I wasn't expecting. I end up gaining a lot of respect for Yatchy in finding out that he's a smart guy who knows the basics of branding yourself, also how to attract an audience to his music and keep that audience coming back. Most artists in Hip Hop just gain publicity on accident and undeservingly roll with it—I mean, we can be honest here, right? There's meaning and passion behind what he does; I'd be a prick not to respect that. Still though, the thought was, what the does this have to do with me? Then the two artists get into an argument, and what started the argument is what made me pause the video and smile. I didn't even pay attention to the rest; I knew why I felt like I should watch that interview, and the smile came from the fact that trusting my intuition never fails:

Lil Yatchy says, "*I am happy every day.*"

"Wait, say that again…" Returns Budden.

"Happy…I am happy…every day because life is moving in such a positive way, I can't get slowed down!"

The tension in the room builds, as the woman and DJ next to these two let them have the floor to themselves.

"So, maybe he has been media-trained." Budden says, as the wrinkles in his forehead show that the anger is building while he points in Yatchy's direction. "This is a very media-trained answer that I am getting."

And after a few words are exchanged between the two that are hard to make out, Budden then conquers center stage with a raising of the voice, as he retorts: "Ok, let me tell you about how humans are: feelings are fickle. What that means is they come and they go. Nobody is one thing forever!" More pointing from Budden, but with a clenched fist this time. "You can not tell me…you would be lying to tell me that, as a young man—how old are you?"

"Nineteen—"

"—In this industry," shouts Budden to cut off further response from Yatchy. "In this industry, in the music business…"

"Mhm."

"You are happy 24/7?" Asks Budden, as this next claim comes with flailing arms and an even more harsh tone than before. "*That is a lie!*"

But is it, really?

The more that I analyzed the situation, I started to think that what I said in the previous chapter was incorrect. I said that it's "nearly impossible to feel happy all the time," as Joe Budden would've agreed with me. But the latter of the argument seemed to become more reasonable as I took a good look at the two of them. Yatchy said he's happy all the time, and his demeanor screamed it enough to where those words didn't necessarily have to leave his mouth if he didn't want them to. The diamond chain he's wearing, the smile on his face, the one that appears to be laughing off Budden's claims...it all points to an individual that truly *does* feel happy. Budden has veins bulging out of his head as he yells, then you look and see that he's wearing an old sweatshirt that looks more beaten down than he does, physically (somehow). He doesn't have as much money as the young man sitting across from him despite being twice his age and famous himself; you start to get the feeling that's the real reason for the anger, not what is being said. Then, I thought about the fact that drama was flocking to Budden at the time, as he nears the end of a career that the tension on his face shows he wishes was still thriving...

I like Budden a lot better as an artist and respect his skill twice as much, but it was hard not to notice how one guy says he believes that he can stay positive 24/7 and his life's circumstances reflected it. The other believes that you must be negative from time to time because it's human nature, and so, his life reflects enormous downswings that're just as big, if not bigger than the ups. The more I continued pondering on it, *they're both right!* Since I've been a believer in Joe Budden's point all this time, my life has had plenty of ups and downs, just like his. Yatchy can control the waves of his mind, while Joe and I have struggled to. And that night I sat there in silence after pausing the interview, reflecting on my own life and how things had been going for me. They weren't even close to as good as I wanted them to be, as I sat and contemplated the fact that the year 2016 held accomplishments and moves for me that were nothing short of incredible, while 2017 was nothing short of a giant letdown in comparison…

Not that I wasn't still successful and enjoying the fact that I turned my life around, but I can be honest and say that I didn't do anything special in terms of success like I planned to. *Warren's Finest* was doing well, but I had already made too many mistakes with the publishing process for it to make as much noise as it should've when I think about the fact that two men with Ivy League, Masters-level degrees in creative writing said the writing was phenomenal during one of the competitions that I entered. I felt myself losing happiness as the book died; 'failure' was the word that I used to describe myself at the time. I always hated myself as a person and felt like the book was all I had left to look forward to, so why should I stay on Earth if it's a failure? I was letting that downward spiral carry into the current moment where I was forgetting to shave or how to write. *Even my job had stopped throwing promotions and raises at me!* And business was always supposed to be the effortless part of my life…

My mother's health had declined and suddenly, she was getting cancer screenings. Amazing networking relationships had turned sour; I suddenly hated working at a place that I had spent every day thankful for the year before. Danny Range had gone from somebody that everybody wished that they could be like to a guy who felt like the world was crashing around him, and he just wasn't ready to admit it to anybody out of pride, so he kept lying on Instagram about how happy he was. It all led to the thought after watching that interview that I want you guys to have and have often: how has my thinking been? Have I been focusing on the right things? Have I been staying positive? If I'm not where I want to be in life, is it because of circumstances that are out of my control, or is it because of me? What happened that made me lose my focus during the good times of my life?

That made me think about the fact that I had just entered a relationship with an amazing girl that I would go on to fall in love with, then I broke up with her because the relationship wasn't as perfect as I imagined. A chance at fame felt like it was inches from my fingertips when *Warren's Finest* began to sell rapidly; I didn't think that I had the time to give that girl the happiness she deserved and so, I left her. Instantly, I regretted it. And my focus shifted from my career and using my success to help other people to "*What have I done?*" Our memories began to be all that I could think about, as I'd spend my nights alone in my room trying to discover that ambition again. I'd eventually break and reach out to her only to be met by a different person, one who resented me instead of imagining what a future with me would be like. I had worked it to the point of where we were going to give it a second chance, and then she found somebody else, who she's currently in a relationship with. The months following the official moment where we ceased all conversation were crushing for me, and I had forgotten everything that I've taught you in this book. Depression sank in deeply, and I even considered quitting my brand, deleting my Instagram, and moving to another state where I could pretend that I hadn't quit on an idea that had the potential to change countless lives.

That "S" word. *Suicide.* So crazy; how dare I even think about it, right? But when you come to the realization that you tossed away the one person that you've always dreamt of having like it was a meaningless piece of trash, how doesn't it cross your mind? I even asked an associate for the gun to do it; I'm lucky the dude lived three hours away from me. If he lived next store, it might've been put to my head and this book wouldn't have existed. I seem so happy all the time, so he would've never guessed what he was handing it to me for. It gives me chills to think about how dark of a place I was truly in…

The waves of positivity left; I let them leave. I let the waves of negativity control me and I continued giving into them, as I experienced another wave of events that came one after another and were almost too much to handle. Injuries that kept me away from the gym, problems with my expensive car that were too much to fix, friendships that were once gold became dramatic and ended for good, and all I did was what most people do, which was to ask myself, "What else could go wrong?" You know what else could wrong? Anything and everything, so long as you continue to feed those negative waves. And as I dropped my tear-filled eyes from the ceiling in that moment where I had forgotten how to write and thought of all this, I said aloud to a room filled with only one presence, my own: "I'm happy for you. I'm sorry, Brooke. I just hope you're happy with him. Best of luck to you both, and I learned my lesson." Then, I felt a wave of positive energy hit me that was more euphoric than any drug I've ever tried, as I picked up my computer and wrote the chapter before this, which went on to be my favorite of the entire book.

Isn't it ironic how the chapter covering the Law of Attraction came when I needed to harness it the most?

Not at all!

If you've been paying attention, you'd know that's how it's supposed to work...

The next day consisted of my most positive, adrenaline-filled day of work in months. I carried that energy and that smile I had forgotten out to my car on my lunch break, where I'd make a call to a principal in Youngstown and land a speech with the board of education for high schools. It will lead to gigs where I'll spread positivity and drug awareness to kids in an area that needs to hear it the most! I went inside and completed a day's work by 2 PM, then emailed the head of alumni at UC where I would land an opportunity to speak at the University, an enormous public school in the Cincinnati area. Within weeks of controlling the positive waves of momentum, I made amends with those friends that I had immaturely started a problem with; I received a text on another day from my mother that said that her tumor was benign, that she'd be able to continue to drive me insane for years to come! Seconds later, I'd receive a call for a job opportunity where it'd later be confirmed that I was the *least-qualified candidate*. I'll never forget that I cut off Nikki in Human Resources mid-sentence, as she was in the middle of telling me that they were still interviewing other people and had forgotten to get back to me...

"I don't give a shit, honestly." I said, with tears in my eyes while staring out a window in an empty meeting room at the office. "Don't get me wrong: I want the opportunity more than anybody and I'll do my best to prove that via hard work if I'm selected out of appreciation for your vote of confidence. However, my mother just passed her cancer screenings, and I have to admit that whether you guys think I'm built for upper-level accounting or not just seems like a very small thing right now..."

(Silence from the other end of the phone.)

"Listen." I continued, but only after laughing aloud. "You called me at an insane time; I apologize if I'm rambling. All I'm saying is best of luck to you guys if it's not me, and if it's not, I'll be ok because I learned to appreciate the small things in life today. My focus is on calling my mother more, not on how much money I can make."

I received a call the next day with a job offer from that woman that included more money than I could've ever imagined I'd make at age twenty-five years old, and I couldn't wait to prove that I was game for the step up in difficulty in terms of my workload. At a moment where the world was literally crashing around me, I had the courage to admit that I was wrong in leaving Brooke and it led to me feeling better about the situation. What I also did in that moment was control those waves of negativity, pick up that computer, and keep fighting for a better day. The circumstances of my life changed almost instantly because of this, including a date with a beautiful blonde being scheduled in Cleveland in a few days for the next step in that part of my life. How do you handle the waves of positive and negative momentum in your own life? Would it hurt to suck it up and admit that there's a good chance that you're making matters worse with your own attitude? And would it really hurt to try and be more positive, even if there's nothing to be positive about? You do want your life's circumstances to change, don't you? If so, why on Earth wouldn't you be willing to try *anything* that can do that for you?

Remember that this is not some fairy-tale; *this is your life.* Positive and negative energy is a real thing and if it's not, how else can you describe why you feel the need to get away from certain people or to leave certain rooms without genuinely having a reason as to why you should? The Law of Attraction, mixed with your intuition, and controlling the waves of positive and negative thoughts are how you write the book on your own future. *What type of book do you want to write?* Do you want to be the person with a salty look on their face that didn't care about what Danny Range had to say? Or are you ready to drop all the tough guy/girl nonsense and start paying attention to people who can help you?

There's one final piece to the Law of Attraction that I'd like to cover, and it's another one of those little Easter eggs you may have missed in this book, as I already mentioned it! What exactly happened when I picked up that phone and had that conversation with the HR lady at my new job? Not that I rambled out of pure emotion, but what did I say? No, not the part where I said that I didn't give a shit. Come on, man. Look closer: "I learned to appreciate the small things in life today."

The Law of Attraction states it clearly and it's the final piece of the puzzle that will allow you to utilize it at your leisure…

You can't get what you want in life unless you appreciate what you already have.

And you have so much more to appreciate in life than you likely believe…

CHAPTER IX:

Appreciate Life as It Is: What Are You Grateful For?

"When I started counting my blessings, my whole life turned around."

Willie Nelson, musician.

Have you ever wondered how some people can wake up in a bed next to their beautiful wife, go downstairs and say goodbye to their amazing children that they love to death, and then get in their luxury car and drive to their high-paying job, yet they're in a terrible mood the entire time that they're working there?

And everyone just lets this slide, too! We, as human beings, completely understand the reasoning behind random, horrible moods from our peers. And we do this because we've all experienced events in our own lives that have caused us to have 'one of those days.' Either you spilled your coffee all over yourself before you opened your eyes fully or the first thing you heard when you woke up in the morning was a loud "Fuck you!" from your girlfriend who finally realized that it's *you* who's eating all the frosted animal crackers, not your kid (she can see the crumbs in your beard, buddy. You're slipping.). Suddenly, that hot wife isn't all that she was cracked up to be when you noticed her for the first time, with that tiny bikini wrapping around that smoking body at the pool, and you spend the entire drive to work hating her existence, instead of smiling about the fact that you're currently driving the vehicle you always wanted or that you cuffed her like you once dreamed of!

If this is you, do you understand how much you're missing out on by *not* looking for reasons to love your life?

Not only is appreciation the final piece to the puzzle that allows you to utilize the Law of Attraction to get what you want out of life, but it introduces you to the anecdote to negativity. The fact of the matter is, whether you're completely broke or can't get laid or can't figure out what you're going to do with the rest of your life, you *do* have things in life to be thankful for, things that are unique to you and you only, and that goes for all of us! As I stated before, the Law tells us that we can't get what we want if we don't appreciate what we already have, so if you're trying to attain happiness in the form of sobriety or money or whatever it may be, you can't do it until you learn the art of gratitude. This is so confusing to some people, and it's completely understandable. One would have the right to question if this works when they're staring hard at their belt buckle that they just bought, thinking about how much they appreciate it, and then they look up and don't see all the groceries that they were hoping would magically appear in their fridge. But those people would only be guilty of failing to apply the final part of being grateful, which is that you need to be grateful for what you *don't* yet have if you want to acquire it!

Don't worry if that last paragraph made you scratch your head, as that's exactly what I did the first time I read into this. But the more I read, the more sense it made. Think about it: what's happening when you appreciate what you already have? You are acknowledging the fact that you have it, yes? *You believe you have it.* You can physically see it, in most cases. And in all the other cases, you can picture having it in your mind since you've had it for some time. You feel good about the fact that you have it, so the Law reacts by doing what it has got to do, which is giving you more of it! The interesting part about how this works is that you would apply the same concept to something that you want to acquire, even if it isn't yours yet…

Think back to a time in your life when you acquired something that you've always wanted. You likely envisioned yourself owning it, and the mere thought of owning it made you feel so happy that you couldn't help but smile. You didn't realize it at the time, but you were on an energy frequency that was giving back to the Law of Attraction thoughts of owning it, since you were visualizing it in your head. Next thing you know, you *did* end up acquiring it. Except you didn't realize that you acquired it by following the Law, you thought it 'just happened.' You visualized, you believed, you felt like it could happen, and it happened. It's just like that old pair of shoes you knew you already owned! You visualized you had them, you believed you still had them, you felt the same way you would feel if you still had them, and as a result, you still had them.

So many people have tried to debunk this, but it's hard to deny. Even the arrogant athlete who never believed for a second that he could lose the championship game did, in fact, have that moment of acceptance that it was possible that he'd lose. Whether that happened before the game and he didn't tell anybody or in the few seconds that he officially did lose it, it didn't matter. He *still believed* that he could lose at some point. He visualized that he could lose, believed that he could lose, began to feel the way that he'd feel if he were about to lose the championship game, and then he found himself hanging his head in defeat as the other team was celebrating their victory. It's as terrifying as it is amazing in the sense that you can control the outcome of your future, so you may feel yourself getting nervous about your thinking moving forward (I know I did at first). You may start to put pressure on yourself to think more positive but remember that the Law works for *every* aspect of life. So, if you're thinking that it's hard to master the Law of Attraction, you will end up attracting circumstances that *do* make it hard to master! The best advice that I can give you is to remember the advice that I gave you, that Rhonda gave me through her amazing work, which is to only try to be positive more often than you're negative, or in this case, appreciative more often than you're not…

A great practice that allows you to beat this into your head is to come to a stop next time you walk into your house or your apartment and look around. Look at everything you own. Think about how amazing it is that you own these things. Your kitchen, your plates, and all the food that go on those plates. Think about how many people around the world would die to be able to own a kitchen like yours. The same goes for people who live with somebody else, as you still own the right to use those utensils and anything else in that home. Think about the clothes on your back, the bed you have, your room and how thankful you are for all of it. Not only will you be attracting circumstances that allow you to always have food to eat, clothes on your back, and a room to shack up in, but you'll learn the most important piece to all of this: how you *feel* when you're thinking that way. At all costs, do this until you know *exactly* how you feel when you're appreciating the things that you already own. Once you've done this enough to where you feel comfortable with it, you can begin to apply that same feeling to the visions in your head of what you want to acquire.

Picture yourself as that slimmed-down, attractive, or sober person that you always wanted to be. Visualize deeply to the point of where you start to feel like you already *are* that person, then apply that appreciative feeling of having it that you'll have become so familiar with. And always keep in mind the example of the athlete who came so close to a championship win when you want to doubt that you'll ever acquire it, as you'll find yourself on the same losing side if you follow in his footsteps. When the battle for what you want gets tough, you simply go back to your appreciation feeling and then walk, talk, and act like it's already yours.

Next thing you know, whenever the Law of Attraction decides that it's time to give you what you believe you already have, then you'll have it. And like the rest of us who have used the Law and seen our dreams slowly but surely come true, you'll be blown away. You'll want to tell *everybody*. You'll *never* want to stop using it. I'll never forget the day that traffic jam stopped happening for good, or the time that I appreciated my relationship with my father and saw it improve, or when I visualized myself speaking in front of live audiences, being known as an awesome author, and using my story to change lives, then saw it all happen before my very own eyes. It's a hilarious game of make believe that's as corny as you might think it is, I promise. But aren't you the open-minded type of person who would give anything a chance if it gave you a shot at your dream, as we addressed before? Then stop thinking so much and start using it!

Smile more.

Love more.

Compliment more.

Tip higher.

Just be happy.

Because the universe will make it worth your while.

So, you've learned the importance of a great routine. You've found your reason why you want to pursue your dream so badly. You've dug deep and found what you're passionate about. You stepped out of your comfort zone and began to embrace the art of change. You've come to an understanding that you need to be confident in yourself. You've learned how to visualize. And then you studied how to apply the Law of Attraction to all of this, so that you have a way to make sure that all of it plays out just as you're hoping it will. Now there's only one piece left to ensure that you have all you need to *Make Success Your Addiction* and see your dreams come true...

It's not only the most important principle that there is, but my favorite one, and the one that *really did* save my life. It's the one part of this book that every example had in common, and what you must embrace to have similar success to all of those mentioned before...

Ladies and gentlemen, you have got to believe yourself.

Believe in your ability to accomplish your goals.

Believe that you're capable of becoming anything you want to be in this world.

It's time to believe.

CHAPTER X:

The Weapon: Believe in Yourself

"Everyone is so offended by the mindset that it takes to be the best in the world."

- "Rowdy" Ronda Rousey, the first woman to be inducted into the UFC Hall of Fame.

THROUGHOUT TIME ITSELF, people have proven time and time again that they are capable of extraordinary things...

From the first caveman to pick up two sticks and rub them together to create fire to the first man setting his feet on the moon, human beings have been defying the odds since we arrived here on Earth. And we will continue to, until some asteroid comes and destroys us all or the Browns win the Super Bowl, and everything just bursts into flames as the clock hits zero (as I run through the streets of Cleveland screaming with happy tears in my eyes).

But how do we do it?

How does the same species that was once dumb enough not to realize that they can create fire for themselves end up landing on the surface of the moon using something created from their own technology?

Simple: *they believed that they could.*

And I want you to read that last sentence over and over until it sinks in, and once you're done, I want you to digest the following stories of some of the most incredible people to ever walk this Earth. I want you to process it all afterward and think about the fact that these people were just like you and I once, until they *decided* to believe that they were capable of the impossible...

The first story begins with a little girl being born in California, but this was no ordinary birth. This little blondie was born with the umbilical cord wrapped around her neck and considered a walking miracle from day one! She developed a speech disorder because of this unfortunate event, and by the age of eight she'd have to deal with something far tougher than strange-sounding dialogue, as her father would commit suicide after breaking his back in a sledding accident. Her mother would then move her to the middle of nowhere in North Dakota, and all to work on that speech disorder that she never asked to have in the first place. A beautiful girl with long, silky blonde hair, but the kids in her high school would never get to see the ugly cauliflower ears that she hid behind that hair, as she was terrified of her own appearance. What she couldn't hide for the life of her was her muscular arms, which led to the unwanted nickname of "Miss Man." By sixteen-years old, Blondie dropped out of high school and moved to Boston to take a career in martial arts seriously, as it had always been a passion of hers. At eighteen-years old, her mother kicked her out of the house for not having a job, yet they would remain close throughout her martial arts career. She'd dedicated her life to the one thing that had never let her down, but she'd finish ninth in her first run at the Olympics, which doesn't exactly help you pay your bills, either...

Depression sunk in, and this unfortunate blonde became doomed, as a wave of negativity that led to drugs and alcohol as a regularity engulfed her, something that's created the same disastrous recipe for anybody who's ever tried to use them to numb their mental pain. By this point, she was living with an older boyfriend who was mentally abusing her because he was too big of a pansy to try and physically abuse the martial arts expert (because of course he was!). She was going through life with no education and no confidence, all while dealing with the horrifying memories of a childhood that even our worst enemies shouldn't have to experience. This all leads to her sleeping in her car due to a lack of a home to call hers, before settling in an apartment with sewage coming out of the toilets. It's a classic example of life starting at the bottom and then hitting what most of us refer to as "rock bottom."

Where would Blondie go from here?

Now, let's pretend that somebody else told you this story, not me. Let's say you're sitting at a bar right now, and this fat guy with a beard comes and sits next to you. He takes a swig of his beer, rubs his gut, and then turns to you and points across the bar at a girl with muscular arms who is attractive otherwise (unless you're into that, I guess). He tells you the same story that I just told you about her, but then proceeds to tell you that one day this girl will go on to become a best-selling author and that, by thirty-years old, she would be a multi-millionaire with her own future in the palm of her hands. You'd start shaking your head and wondering why the hell he's telling you all this, wouldn't you?

And then he'd start to tell you that she'll also end up being one of the most famous female athletes in the history of planet Earth. That she'd star in movies, be on late night television shows, and that one day a sport started only for men's participation would be *begging her* to continue to headline their events; she'll become their most-prized asset. You'd probably proceed to pretend that you were getting a phone call so that you could leave your seat and never sit next to this crazy man again! Funny thing is, the type of man that understands the art of believing in yourself would know something that you might not, in this case, and he'd want to know more about the girl. And he'd want to know more because he understands that the person sitting across from you *is* capable of great things and the only reason that you're not is because you aren't open-minded to the possibility that normal people can become inspirations if they simply believe that they can.

If you haven't picked it up by now, you've likely been living under a rock for the last five years; that story is true, and that little girl with a speech impediment that I called "Blondie" goes by the name of *Ronda Rousey*. When the world told Ronda that she wasn't anything special, that she couldn't overcome adversity and become the first female champion in the history of the UFC, she curved her eyebrows downward in irritation, decided that she believed in herself, and continued pushing towards her dreams until people like me were writing books on her and being completely inspired by her mere existence. The difference between Ronda and normal people is that Ronda believed, *do you believe?*

How about the story of the foreign man who came to the United States to chase his dream of being an actor and writing his own screenplays? He was told he looked and talked funny, that it was impossible for him to ever be a 'big-name actor.' This ogre looking son-of-a-gun had to sleep in bus stations as a homeless man because he was lacking the funds for his own pad. So, yeah, one could say he was far from five-star dinners and sleeping with models in Hollywood! He even admits that he went to the liquor store and tried to sell his dog to any stranger he saw because he couldn't afford to feed it! (Yikes...) Ogre would end up somehow affording to go to a boxing match where he'd get an idea for an amazing story, then he'd go home (the bus station) to look for a way to write this masterpiece developing in his mind. After finding a way to complete it, he'd receive an offer for that story for around $125,000 or so and decline it because he wouldn't be able to star in the movie like he dreamed! After taking the official offer to star in the movie for $35,000, he bought the dog back for $25,000 from the guy that he sold it to, and that story he wrote went on to become one of the greatest stories ever told. *Rocky* was its name, perhaps you've heard of it? (I ask with as much sarcasm as I could possibly be allowed to put here...) Sylvester Stallone believed in his vision, and he still believed when his poor dog was being shopped around the black market like a crispy bag of crack, so why wouldn't *you* believe that you're capable of incredible things?

Do you think JK Rowling waited for permission to believe in herself when she was sending the manuscript for *Harry Potter* around to publishers and getting denied? What else could she possibly do when she was fired from her job and had to consider welfare as a poor single mother? JK kept fighting until she was a billionaire, that's nine zeroes. *Nine.* She went from jobless and welfare to a billion dollars, all because she believed that a story about a wizard was destined to be heard around the world. Now the rest of us writers scour the internet for her contact information and beg her to acknowledge that we're great as well. Do you think the lot of us would've done that the day after she lost her job? *Why not?* Was the story she held in her hands that day not the same as the one we all went on to be fascinated by? What do you think led to that story becoming what is was, as she was stuck in that position? A belief in herself when all the odds were against her, when her employer didn't even think she had the intelligence to hold a normal desk job. JK Rowling still believed in herself, *so why don't you believe?* What's different about the position you're in now and the position she was in when she lost her job? What's the difference between anybody struggling to make ends-meat and that single mother with a writing dream?

Walt Disney still believed when he was told that he had no creativity. Robert Downey Jr believed when he was face down in a pool of blood in prison, having been beaten half to death for no reason after he was thrown behind bars for driving naked under the influence of drugs. *The guy caught the attention of police for throwing imaginary rats out of his car!* Although, RDJ still had it in the back of his mind that he was going to be a globally-known actor. Robert Downey Jr got out of that cell and fought until little kids idolized him, until they wanted to grow up one day and be like *The Ironman.* Do you think that they would've thought that way if they were introduced to him when he was sitting in a jail cell? *Why not?* It's the same man, the same talent, just at a different place in his life. They love him now because he believed in himself. People like me love him now because I understand that stories like his are the reason that anybody can go from any position in life to something great, so long as they believe. Even if you *are* reading this in a cell right now, *who's to say that you can't get out and become a somebody?* You can rise from the ashes like RDJ, but only if you believe in yourself the same way that he did…

Ronda Rousey was a normal person with problems that a lot of you can relate to, but *she believed* that she was capable of extraordinary things. Stallone was a normal person with problems that a lot of you can relate to, but *he believed* that he was capable of extraordinary things. Walt Disney was a normal person with problems that a lot of you can relate to, but *he believed* that he was capable of extraordinary things. Robert Downey Jr was a normal person with problems that a lot of you can relate to, but *he believed* that he was capable of extraordinary things. These are the people the rest of the world wants to be like, but those people fail to realize that they *are* just like them! They're in their shoes, but they're at the crossroads; they haven't made it to the glory yet. And those people have a decision to make. Better yet, *you* have a decision to make. When the world tells you that you can't do something—that you're a loser because you're jobless, that you're a bum because you're homeless, or that you're a scumbag because you've been to prison—will you take their word for it, lay down, and die? Or will you get up and write your own ending to the story?

I want you to get up write that story, homie.

Furthermore, I want you to shoot for the stars like Ronda, JK, Stallone, Disney, and RDJ. I wrote this entire book with the thought in mind that you guys may only want to pursue a small goal, but I couldn't finish it without pointing out to you just how much you could accomplish if you really wanted to. I wanted this book to pave its way like something of a roadmap for you guys, so that you could come to this point seeing that the winners of today all use these same core techniques to achieve what they achieve. There's absolutely *nothing* wrong with starting small. There's absolutely *nothing* wrong with a normal life. I can see why people don't chase what I'm chasing the older I get but imagine what the world would be like if *everybody* understood the type of power that they could harness by *believing* that they can achieve anything that they set their mind to!

How many movies are lost in the minds of future writers who didn't think that it was possible for them to write?

How many doctors end up working in fast food because they didn't believe that it was possible for them to get through medical school? How many legendary athletes end up watching the games at home for the rest of their lives because they gave up when they were cut from the high school team, instead of trying harder like Michael Jordan did when his school cut him?

I don't want this to be you.

I want you to be the next genius investor. I don't want you to stop at getting clean; I want you write books about it, have a movie be made about your life, and then have you headline an event that I'll be *begging* to speak at. I want you to become the literary agent that *I'm praying* will find interest in my future projects. I want you invent the next great gadget or delicious food recipe. I want you to be able to accomplish every hope and dream that has ever entered your mind. And when you do, I don't want you to tell the world that it was because of Danny Range…

I want you to tell them that it was because you believed in yourself.

And when they ask you to elaborate on all your incredible success, I want you to tell them the same way that I have been telling them for the last three years: If you believe…if you believe that you can do anything...if you believe that you can do anything that you set your damn mind to, then you can.

And once you do, then this world is yours for the taking...

JUST BELIEVE!!!!!

CHAPTER XI:

Conclusion: The Dream Sheet

I once heard about a book where someone named it something along the lines of 'How to have a sex life in your 60s' and the book was filled with empty pages because there is no sex life in your 60s! Now, I want to meet that guy/gal because that's hilarious and even more so, genius. But I'm not here to steal your money by making you do the work involved with this book by yourself. Plus, another reason that I'm not a fan of the usual 'how-to' book is because it leaves too many unanswered questions! Most intelligent people ask questions as they take in information, but how the heck you supposed to get ahold of the author for every question you have? I didn't want you to learn what I've taught you, have some questions, and end up quitting because I wasn't there to tell you how to work the kinks out! So, what better to do than leave you something at the end that allows you to apply all the information that you've just learned?

The rest of this book will have a set of directions along with spaces left for you to write your answers to each of the scenarios in question, also how you plan to go about carrying out everything I just taught you in real life. So, grab a pen and get creative! To make it easier, I will fill this out myself so that you have an example to go by. I'm one of you, as I mentioned in the intro, so know that I'm keeping this book next to my bed to follow along just like you will be. And remember that success is not a race, it's a marathon. Some goals take years, some take days. Your goal will take as long as it needs to; you need to be ready for that. Use the official manual you're about to create for yourself to get there!

I call it "The Dream Sheet."

As you'll have no choice but to achieve your dreams if you take the time to complete it and stick to it…

Your Routine

Our first principal points out that you've got to be organized if you want any of this to work, so we'll start with the easy ground ball. Each day of the week will be listed below, and you'll use the space provided to create a schedule for yourself. There are twenty-four hours in a day; you will account for every hour in this schedule as if your life depended upon it, including how many hours you assume that you'll sleep, the hours you plan to work, the hours it'll take to exercise, etc. Also, there's nothing wrong with taking time off from it from time to time. For God's sake, don't call your mother on her death bed to tell her you that couldn't be there because Danny Range's schedule told you that you can't miss your 10 AM exercise. But I highly recommend sticking to this schedule until it becomes routine to you. If you try it for a few weeks and then quit for a few more weeks, it's never going to feel normal. Suck it up, write it, participate in what you wrote, get used to it, and enjoy the results that it is promised to bring to your life.

Danny:
Monday:
7 AM: Wake up, get dressed, and drive to my day job.
8 AM – 12 PM: Participate in the necessary activities of my day job.

12 PM – 1 PM: Study/eat lunch/do homework for my MBA program (grad school), as I won't have time to do this later at night.
1 PM – 5 PM: Participate in the necessary activities of my day job.
5 PM – 6:15 PM: Drive to the gym and exercise, as the extra fifteen-minute window accounts for the usual traffic in Columbus.
6:15 PM – 7 PM: Drive home and shower, as an extra fifteen minutes is accounted for in case of traffic.
7 PM – 8 PM: Make dinner, as I meal prep for breakfast and lunch the following day, then I post on Instagram.
8 PM – 9:30 PM: Eat dinner, then use this time to either watch sports, network for my speaking career, or write my book. But now this is book is done! Looks like it's time to write another...
9:30 PM – 10:30 PM: Call/text mother, brother, father, other family, or friends and then spend the rest of the night reading some type of motivational/positivity book to prep for the next day.
10:30 PM: Goodnight.

Tuesday:
7 AM: Same as Monday.
8 AM – 12 PM: Same as Monday.
12 PM – 1 PM: Same as Monday.
1 PM – 5 PM: Same as Monday.
5 PM – 6:15 PM: Same as Monday.
6:15 PM – 7 PM: Same as Monday.
7 PM – 8 PM: Same as Monday.

8 PM – 9:30 PM: Same as Monday.
9:30 PM – 10:30 PM: Same as Monday.
10:30 PM: Goodnight.

Wednesday:
7 AM: Same as Monday.
8 AM – 12 PM: Same as Monday.
12 PM – 1 PM: Either have lunch with a co-worker or leave the office to drive in circles and listen to music for an hour. I do *not* touch the books on Wednesday.
1 PM – 5 PM: Same as Monday.
5 PM – 6 PM: Drive home and shower, as this is an off day from working out to let my body rest. This is an hour to account for heavier traffic, since I'm on the highway at rush hour.
6 PM – 7 PM: Have dinner with a friend to socialize or go out to eat by myself to clear my head.
7 PM – 8 PM: Watch SportsCenter, then post on Instagram.
8 PM – 10 PM: Watch a movie, sporting event, or participate in more plans with friends.
10 PM – 10:30 PM: Call/text with the family or more friends.
10:30 PM: Goodnight.

Thursday:
7 AM: Same as Monday.
8 AM – 12 PM: Same as Monday.
12 PM – 1 PM: Same as Monday.
1 PM – 5 PM: Same as Monday.
5 PM – 6:15 PM: Same as Monday.

6:15 PM – 7 PM: Same as Monday.
7 PM – 8 PM: Same as Monday.
8 PM – 9:30 PM: Same as Monday.
9:30 PM – 10:30 PM: Same as Monday.
10:30 PM: Goodnight.

Friday:
7 AM: Same as Monday.
8 AM – 12 PM: Same as Monday.
12 PM – 1 PM: Same as Monday.
1 PM – 5 PM: Same as Monday.
5PM – 6:15 PM: Same as Monday.
6:15 PM – 7 PM: Same as Monday.
7 PM – 8 PM: Same as Monday.
8 PM – 12 AM: Oh, Friday nights are always for writing; they have been since I was nineteen!
12 AM: Goodnight.

Saturday:
9 AM – 10 AM: Late wake up to catch up on rest, mentally *and* physically! Then, I eat breakfast and head to the gym.
10 AM – 11:15 AM: Exercise, with travel time accounted for.
11:15 AM – 3 PM: Get home, shower, eat lunch, and then get the next week's school work done ahead of time so I'll be able to maintain this schedule (I won't have time for schoolwork during the week nights, as it interferes with the rest of what is scheduled).
3 PM – 3 AM: Whatever the hell I want! You have got to get out and live a little, right? Maybe I'll go out to eat,

experience something new in the city, or go out and catch up with friends. But whatever I do, I am *not* thinking about anything productive. A schedule this intense would cause you to overload if you don't take some time off every now and then. Trust me, I've crashed before…

Sunday:
11 AM – 12 PM: Wake up, shower, eat brunch, and start the laundry.
12 PM – 2 PM: Create the posts for the next week on Instagram and then download them to my phone, also finish the laundry.
2 PM – 5 PM: Always some type of reading or writing.
5 PM – 10 PM: Eat dinner, then do whatever I want for the rest of the night. I'll usually head out to my father's house to catch up with his family before coming home, getting ready for bed, and then proceeding to go to sleep and start it all over again on Monday.

Keep in mind that things like family time, socializing, or how much time you take to yourself is entirely up to you! I encourage you to make sure that it's all involved in the schedule though, as you could end up losing those people if you stick to yourself too much. It's a mistake that I made early on while creating my own schedule, but one that I hope my experience can stop you from making yourself.

You:

Monday:

Tuesday:

Wednesday:

Thursday:

Friday:

Saturday:

Sunday:

Why

THINK BACK TO the second chapter or re-read it on your own time if you need to. If you don't have a reason to get out of bed and pursue your goals, then it'll get increasingly harder to do so each day. I want you to fill the rest of this blank page with the reason *why* you feel the need improve every aspect of your life, then I want you to come back and read what you wrote any time you feel like quitting on yourself. If you still feel like quitting after you read this on a bad day, then you need to think long and hard about whether it's the right 'why' or not. There is nothing wrong with writing multiple things on this page, either, or changing what your 'why' is until you find one that works for you…

Danny:

The reason why I want to fight for a better life is because I have a family to take care of. I have an amazing mother who sacrificed her interests in life for me, as well as a brother that needs a solid role model to look up to. I have zero reason not to treat today like it is my game seven of the World Series.

You:

The reason why I want to fight for a better life is because

____

____

Passion

CHAPTER THREE TELLS us that we'll get bored with our routine if we don't involve something we love to do in our daily lives. You'll notice that most of my time is spent at my day job, but anybody who knows me personally will tell you that I can't stand accounting! I do it for the money it gives me, so that I can use it to fund my Process. The way I make sure I don't go insane is to make sure that I'm always writing, posting about speaking, or socializing with my friends so that I have something to look forward to everyday!

You're going to use the following page to make a promise to yourself. You have something that you're passionate about, and if you don't, we'll use the first question to allow you time to think about it until something clicks. Next, you're going to write out how you're going to use your Process to make sure that you chase that dream career, or if it isn't a career, then you're going to write out how that passion is going to make you the happiest and richest version of yourself possible. This ties in with our visualizing and the Law of Attraction, as writing this out and believing in it leaves you no choice but to make it a reality.

Danny:

What are you passionate about?

I have always had passions for story-telling and helping others.

How are you going to incorporate that passion into your Process?

I will make sure that—no matter how crazy my schedule is—I always do something each day that pushes me towards my dream of being a globally-known author, entrepreneur, and public speaker. And whether that's five minutes or ten hours, it doesn't matter. I will *always* make sure I am chasing that goal in some way.

You:

What are you passionate about?

____

____

____

____

____

____

How are you going to incorporate that passion into your Process?

____

____

____

____

____

____

Step Out of Your Comfort Zone

The chapter on change teaches us that we mustn't be afraid to embrace getting over our fears if we are to develop the courage to chase our dreams. Nothing will make you more confident than conquering a fear that has been holding you back your entire life! Use this page to admit to your fears and make another important promise to yourself, one that will help you get over them for good and awaken a level of confidence that you weren't aware that you had...

Danny:

What are you afraid of?

I'm afraid to speak in front of crowds. I'm afraid to approach women in public if I'm not under the influence of drugs. I'm afraid of not living up to my potential.

What are you going to do about it?

I'm going to practice public speaking every day—whether it be online, in my room, or in front of others—until I am phenomenal at it. I will continue improving at this skill until I'm making more money doing it than I already do at my full-time accounting job. I'm also going to force myself to go out once a week and introduce myself to a woman that I've never met before (if I'm single), and I'll do this until my social anxiety goes away completely. Lastly, I'm going to stick to my Process and continuing growing my brand until I'm one of the most successful people to have ever been born in Warren, Ohio. And if I'm not able to do this, then I'll just have to die in the act of trying.

You:

What are you afraid of?

____

____

____

____

____

____

What are you going to do about it?

____

____

____

____

____

____

Confidence

Recall the example of Conor McGregor and how he declared himself the future of combat sports before he had any right to. The chapter on confidence tells us that we must believe we are capable of big things before we have any chance to be and we will use this page to build that type of supreme confidence! And I want you to forget the word arrogant for a moment; I want you to embrace what some may call 'cocky.' You will be provided a space to tell the world who you believe you are, then you're going to stick to your Process until you become that person…

Don't you dare hold back.

Danny:
Hello, ladies and gentlemen. My name is Danny Range. Depression isn't a thing to me, as it can't affect my life in a negative manner. I'm one of the greatest creative minds this world has ever seen. And EVERYONE in this world is going to know my name before I turn forty.

You:
Hello, ladies and gentlemen. My name is

____

____

____

____

Visualization

I USED JORDAN Belfort's famous office speech to teach you how to use your dream triggers, so that you can create a picture of yourself in your mind that forces you to be hungry enough to chase that vision. Instead of talking about it, this page will ask the question that allows you to create that picture. And after you answer the following question, I want you to sit wherever you are and close your eyes for as long as you're comfortable doing so. Visualize what you wrote on the paper. Remember to *feel* like you're living in that moment. Breathe it. *Be it.* And remember that feeling for life, as you're on your way to experiencing it in real life if you're willing to work at it hard enough.

Danny:
Where will you be in ten years?

In ten years, I will be an entrepreneur who has expanded his business into multiple states. I will be using the money that I saved from my business career and investments to expand my brand around the world, as speaking opportunities will be coming to me at this point; I won't have to work so hard for them. I'll have been signed to an agent as a writer, as my brand will begin to catch the attention of Hollywood producers who will consider investing into my stories for book-to-film transitions. As all of this is happening, I'll be working on my dream TV-series, getting ready to pursue a major deal via Netflix or HBO. Most importantly, I won't have to swear to the world that these things are going to happen; they'll assume that they're in the works because they'll have already heard my name thrown around publicly. My family won't have to work if they don't want to; they'll have been taken care of financially.

You:

Where will you be in ten years?

The Law of Attraction

REMEMBER THAT THE Law of Attraction is always working, as it's one with the universe. And since the Law is always working, we must be monitoring our thoughts if we are to attract the life that we want. You received the bigger explanation in the chapters dedicated to this, but we're going to simplify it here by allowing you to begin using its three easy steps. It goes in this order: Ask, believe, attain. You must send out the signal to the universe that you want to acquire something, then you convince yourself that you have it already, you feel like you have it already, and then you attain it. Use the following page to follow those three steps and begin the process...

Danny:

Ask: I want to become a famous author, entrepreneur, and public speaker who uses his wealth to take care of his family and give back to his community.

Believe: My name is Danny Range, and I am a famous author, entrepreneur, and public speaker who *used* his wealth to take care of his family and give back to his community.

Attain: I am so grateful that I became a famous author, entrepreneur, and public speaker who saw all his life-long dreams come true.

You:

Ask:

Believe:

Attain:

Control Your Waves

The chapter on handling negativity told us that the worst parts of our lives come to us because of our attitude and thinking, just the like positive things, and that's because the law works both ways. I want you to use this page to list the best things that have ever happened to you, then I want you to make a pact to yourself that you will never dwell on the bad parts of your past again.

Any time that you experience 'one of those days,' you can come back to this page and stare at this list of amazing events that you have put together. Then, you will go back to your visualization techniques, so that you can put yourself back in time to the exact moment that those amazing things happened to you. In mere moments, you will feel negativity leave your body and you'll be ready to proceed on with the rest of your day. Once you've practiced this with the paper enough, you will come to a point where you don't need the book and can instantly put yourself back into that positive state of mind on your own! I can't wait until that happens for you; it's essential to the people around you and yourself! (Mine may be long, but yours can be one sentence. Whatever brings up the memory easiest!)

Danny:

What are the best moments of your life?

I'll never forget when the Cleveland Cavs won the NBA Finals and my friend offered me a shot after the final seconds ticked off the clock. It was the first time since I had been introduced to substance that I willingly turned it down. That moment was the beginning of my sobriety, and the beginning of my journey towards real happiness. I don't know if I'd still be here if it weren't for that team winning that year. Thank you, LeBron James, for everything that you did for Northeast Ohio!

My little league coach would never let me pitch. He used to promise me; he even let me warm up in the bullpen a few times only to never let me in the game! My dad made me change leagues because of this and I'd end up developing amazing skills as a pitcher elsewhere. As a senior in high school, my team played our rivals, a school full of kids that I used to play in the first little league with. We were the smallest school in the area, and they were ranked in the top twenty-five in the state at the time. I pitched the entire game and ended up hitting a walk off shot to the fence that gave us the victory. That moment of the ball leaving my bat is still vivid in my mind! How's that taste, Coach Doan? (A joke, of course. He's a great guy, and I ended up being close friends with his kid.)

Walking across the stage at my college graduation and seeing my mother, father, and brother so proud will always hold a special place in my heart. People doubted that my parents could raise a child since they had me when they were just teenagers. I know that moment was a lot bigger for them than it was for me, and I'm so proud of the job they did guiding me to keep my head on straight despite my substance abuse problems.

(A good cheat is to have little reminders to carry around with you. I have plenty of Cincinnati clothing, as it always brings up that memory of graduating when I wear it. I kept a 'Cavs 2016 Finals Champions' sticker on my car, so I can see it and be reminded of that moment every morning. I also keep my high school baseball plaque in my room, which has a reminder from my coach about that great game engraved: "Warren Catholic-6 Warren Public-5.")

You:

What are the best moments of your life?

Gratitude

THE CHAPTER ABOUT appreciation explains that being grateful is what teaches you how to truly feel like you've attained what you want already. And you can't do this if you don't first learn how to be grateful for the things that you already have. I don't care if you're homeless; I don't care if you're a junkie. You have things in life to be thankful for! And you're going to prove that to yourself by listing as many of them as you possibly can on this page. I'll keep mine short, but I encourage you to fill every corner of every blank page or blank portion of other pages in this book if you can. Just remember what it feels like to be grateful for those things, as you'll then use whatever space you have left to say that you're grateful for the things you want but don't have yet. When you write those, be sure to force upon yourself that same grateful feeling and carry that feeling until you physically see that you have those things.

Danny:
What are you grateful for?

Thank you, universe, for the happiness and good health of my friends, family, and myself.

Thank you, universe, for my amazing and perfectly-functioning, brand new Chevy Malibu.

Thank you, universe, for allowing me to find my beautiful blonde wife with a great ass…personality (winks). Darn auto-correct!

Thank you, universe, for allowing me to become a famous author, entrepreneur, and public speaker.

Thank you, universe, for allowing to me take care of my family financially.

Thank you, universe, for allowing all my dreams to come true.

You:

What are you grateful for?

____

Just Believe

NOW LET'S JUST keep this last one short and self-explanatory!

Danny:
My name is Danny Range, and I believe in myself.

You:

____

____

____

Best of luck to you!

Now go out and *Make Success Your Addiction...*

And once again, when you attain everything that you've ever wanted in life using your Process, be sure to tell the world that it happened because you believed in yourself. I'll always be here fighting for a better life, just as I expect you to. So, better yet, let's tell them together, just like the Law says that we should (in advance): #WeBelieved.

Made in the USA
Middletown, DE
29 June 2019